JOSEPH, THE MAN WHO RAISED JESUS

JOSEPH
THE MAN WHO RAISED JESUS

Fr. Gary Caster

servant
AN IMPRINT OF
FRANCISCAN MEDIA
Cincinnati, Ohio

Unless otherwise noted, Scripture passages have been taken from the *Revised Standard Version*, Catholic edition. Copyright 1946, 1952, 1971 by the Division of Christian Education of the National Council of Churches of Christ in the USA. Used by permission. All rights reserved. Quotes are taken from the English translation of the *Catechism of the Catholic Church* for the United States of America (indicated as *CCC*), 2nd ed. Copyright 1997 by United States Catholic Conference—Libreria Editrice Vaticana.

Book and cover design by Mark Sullivan
Cover image © Peter Wm. Gray, S.S., Ph.D

Library of Congress Cataloging-in-Publication Data
Caster, Gary, 1961-
Joseph, the man who raised Jesus / Fr. Gary Caster.
pages cm
ISBN 978-1-61636-553-0
1. Joseph, Saint. I. Title.
BS2458.C28 2013
232.9ʾ32—dc23
2013013725

ISBN 978-1-61636-553-0

Published by Servant, an imprint of Franciscan Media.
28 W. Liberty St.
Cincinnati, OH 45202
www.FranciscanMedia.org

Printed in the United States of America.

Prayer to Jesus of the Hidden Years in Nazareth

O my Jesus, much of your life is hidden within the Immaculate
Heart of Mary,

so I ask that you place me there.

Let your mother, together with St. Joseph,

shape my life according to the community of love in your
home at Nazareth,

Let me learn everything they taught you so that the ordinary
responsibilities of my life will manifest the extraordinary
love that is your enduring gift to the human family.

Let the secret memories of your time at home guide my
thoughts, strengthen my heart, and direct my actions.

Teach me to be content wherever I am and with whatever you
have asked me to do.

Help me to be always confident of that which you have given
me,

ever enthusiastic to serve you in others,

and every day grateful.

O Lord, show me that I do not need to be noticed, accepted,
praised, celebrated, or consulted;

that I do not need anything but to remain at home with you,
your mother, and St. Joseph. Amen.

For my mother,
Nancy L. Caster
Thank you for sharing your friendship with
and your love for
St. Joseph

CONTENTS

M Y MOTHER RAISED MY SISTERS and brothers and me in the Catholic faith. While my father supported her "nonnegotiable" decision, he wasn't baptized until just before my seventeenth birthday. That was an extremely moving day for all of us, especially my mother. She had never forced my father to believe, but she did provide him with an outstanding example of what it means to be a person of faith and service.

Because of the way my mother lived her faith, going to church was a natural and normal part of our lives and never merely a duty or an obligation. Life in the parish was simply an extension of our life at home. Dad would often complain that Mom spent more time at church than at home, that she took better care of the priests than she did of her family. Yet he was always teasing. He was proud of the woman he had married.

Dad, too, would later become involved in service to the Church. I can still remember the first time he stood next to me to help distribute Holy Communion. And how proud and overwhelmed I was when he called to tell me that he and my mother would be taking Communion to the housebound and the dying. This wasn't too long after he buried his youngest child, my sister, who died at age thirty-six.

My mother met my father at a wedding reception. She had been saying a novena to St. Joseph to help her find a spouse, and when she first laid eyes on my father, she knew at once that he was the man God intended for her. And she was right; my parents have been married for fifty-four years. Even now my mother will gladly tell you that it was St. Joseph who brought the two of them together.

St. Joseph has always been my mother's favorite saint. He was her patron when she was growing up: her guardian, provider, teacher, and father. Joseph quite literally raised her in the faith. As a child she would go to Mass with only Joseph accompanying her. Through his prodding she told her parents that she wanted to be confirmed and attend the Catholic high school. Joseph instilled within my mother the courage to explain how important her faith was to her and to confidently express it. Today my mother will happily tell you that St. Joseph told her that colon cancer wouldn't kill her and that he now helps her with her failing memory.

It is little surprise that when our family moved to Orange County we settled in at St. Joseph parish. All five of us children attended the grade school; went regularly to Mass, confession, and adoration; and enjoyed what was arguably our second home.

Mom would speak openly to St. Joseph, just as if he was physically with us in the house. She was so at ease with the friendship they shared that I never thought such behavior strange. It wasn't until I was much older that I realized that many Catholics don't live the communion of saints the way my mother does and the way she taught us to.

Through my mother's relationship with St. Joseph, I learned that the great fellowship of Christ's companions that now share life with him are present to us in the mystical body of Christ. They can challenge, encourage, comfort, and care for us to the extent that we let them. The saints are real friends to us; their presence in our lives is a great gift of God to which we do well to make recourse. They are alive in Christ, and they share his desire to gather the whole world to him.

My mother encouraged all her children to find at least one close saintly friend and hold fast to that person for life. Mine is St. Thérèse of Lisieux. We have been friends since I was in the fourth grade.

I've long wanted to write a book about St. Joseph for my mother. When I first began sharing with people this hope, many of them asked how such a project could be possible. Over and over again I was told, "But he never says a word," and, "We know so little about him."

While it's true that the Scriptures record no spoken words of Joseph, all four Gospel authors make reference to him, and Luke and Matthew speak of him directly. On two key occasions Matthew goes so far as to tell us what Joseph is thinking and feeling: He "considered" whether to send his pregnant betrothed away quietly (Matthew 1:20), and "he was afraid to go" back to Judea, a fear that an angel confirmed in a dream as justifiable (Matthew 2:22).

Joseph is an icon of our faith precisely because there are no recorded words of his. I believe that words would be a distraction. His love of Our Lady, care for Jesus, obedience, faith, purity, simplicity, courage, and hope speak loudly from the home he built in Nazareth. Joseph is the headmaster of that home school.

And I believe that we know a great deal about St. Joseph—more than if he had penned a Gospel of his own—from the person he raised, a man we know a great deal about. The descriptions of St. Joseph's life and character that follow, while rooted in the Scripture passages that mention him, are chiefly inspired by Jesus's teachings. For some thirty years Jesus lived, prayed, celebrated, studied, and shared in the home Joseph established. The years in Nazareth were a real foundation upon which Jesus would build his saving ministry. St. Joseph is best known through Jesus's words and deeds.

St. Joseph was the man who risked everything to care for Mary and her son, safeguarding them from harm and cherishing them with the purest love. His life is thus a catechism writ large, a flesh-and-blood testimony of what it means to live according to the Father's will, with one's mind and heart centered on Christ. And in him we also see a man with a wholesome Marian spirituality.

There are three critical moments of Joseph's life recorded in Scripture: the time of his betrothal to Mary, the moment he learns she is with child, and the revelation in Joseph's dream about her condition. Each offers a glimpse of the natural virtues of this laborer and upstanding Jewish man, the carpenter who will build something beautiful for the God of his forefathers. These moments teach us about the transition from the old Law to the new and its resulting hope. They also indicate the shift that must occur in our own lives when God asks us to do the unimagined.

Historically speaking, Joseph is the father of the new covenant of God's love and thus possesses an insight into the work of God that complements that of Mary. We can say then that Joseph doesn't merely raise Jesus according to the Father's plan: Joseph raises every Christian. He is rightly called the patron of the Universal Church because the attentive care he exercised on behalf of Mary and Jesus he continues to lavish upon us. He loves the precious bride whom Jesus will one day present to the Father in heaven. He longs to help us live and express our faith, just as he helped my mother.

I encourage you to look at St. Joseph, to gaze upon this man who lived in such close proximity to our Lord. You will find a window that opens to the divine in vibrant ways.

As my mother knew, St. Joseph has much to teach us.

CHAPTER ONE

THE SPOUSE OF MARY

Husbands, love your wives, as Christ loved the Church and gave himself up for her, that he might sanctify her, having cleansed her by the washing of water with the word, that he might present the Church to himself in splendor, without spot or wrinkle or any such thing, that she might be holy and without blemish. Even so husbands should love their wives as their own bodies. He who loves his wife loves himself. For no man ever hates his own flesh, but nourishes and cherishes it, as Christ does the Church, because we are members of his body. (Ephesians 5:25–30)

OUR UNDERSTANDING OF JOSEPH'S BETROTHAL and subsequent marriage to Mary is couched within the opening lines of St. Matthew's Gospel (1:1–18). Although these verses are generally used to explain Jesus's heritage, they are also the genealogy of St. Joseph. Starting with Abraham, Matthew moves the reader through the history of God's covenant with the human family—person by person—up to "Joseph, the husband of Mary" (1:16).

What Matthew has preserved is much more than Joseph's extended family history. By moving us through important biblical relationships, Matthew introduces us to Joseph in continuity with the covenant God established with Abraham centuries before. Thus, by the end of this genealogy, it should be clear that Joseph, as well as everything in

Matthew's Gospel, is meant to be understood within the framework of covenant. Matthew tethers the life of Joseph not simply to Mary and Jesus but, inventively, to all humanity. The names he gives recount in shorthand the legacy of God's saving love. This saving love, "God's covenant with Israel," the prophets often presented in "the image of… faithful married love" (*CCC*, 1611).

> For your Maker is your husband,
>> the LORD of hosts is his name;
> and the Holy One of Israel is your Redeemer,
>> the God of the whole earth he is called. (Isaiah 54:5)

St. Luke, on the other hand, wants us to appreciate St. Joseph in the light of God's intention from the beginning. He traces the family line all the way back to "Adam, son of God" (see Luke 3:23–28). Luke wants us to consider Joseph and his betrothal to Mary in relation to the first couple, Adam and Eve, the backdrop of the election of Abraham and God's subsequent covenant with the people of Israel.

The first chapter of sacred Scripture affirms and reaffirms the truth of our being created in the image and likeness of God:

> God said, "Let us make man in our image, after our likeness; and let them have dominion over the fish of the sea, and over the birds of the air, and over the cattle, and over all the earth, and over every creeping thing that creeps upon the earth." So God created man in his own image, in the image of God he created him; male and female he created them. And God blessed them, and God said to them, "Be fruitful and multiply, and fill the earth and subdue it; and have dominion over the fish of the sea and over the birds of the air and over every living thing that moves upon the earth." (Genesis 1:26–28)

"Male and female he created them": This fundamental truth is further underscored in the second chapter of Genesis, when God declares, "It is not good that the man should be alone" (2:18). With these few words God establishes love as the essential and intrinsic vocation of every human being. God intends the mutual love of man and woman to be an indissoluble union expressing his own unconditional and unyielding love for the human family (see *CCC*, 1604, 1605). Thus the mystery of God's life is uniquely and inextricably bound to the original communion of man and woman that God established in the beginning.

By presenting Joseph's life within the context of God's covenant with man and the truth of human origins, the Gospels remind us that the union of man and woman should never be considered a merely human institution. What God had in mind from the beginning remains within the nature of man and woman, even after the disruption of original sin. Jesus confirmed this:

> Have you not read that he who made them from the beginning made them male and female, and said, "For this reason a man shall leave his father and mother and be joined to his wife, and the two shall become one"? So they are no longer two but one. What therefore God has joined together, let no man put asunder. (Matthew 19:4–6).

Loving communion remains the hallmark of human life. "The order of creation persists, though seriously disturbed" (*CCC*, 1608).

Only God can heal the disorder of sin. At the moment of the original rejection of his will, God promises to extend himself to the human family in a way that will call us back to the truth of our origins and the fullness of our humanity:

The LORD God said to the serpent,
"... I will put enmity between you and the woman,
   and between your seed and her seed;
he shall bruise your head,
   and you shall bruise his heel." (Genesis 3:14, 15).

This is precisely why God later establishes a covenant relationship with Abraham.

> Indeed, "the economy of the Old Testament was deliberately so oriented that it should prepare for and declare in prophecy the coming of Christ, redeemer of all men." ... [T]he books of the Old Testament bear witness to the whole divine pedagogy of God's saving love. (*CCC*, 122).[1]

Matthew's genealogy lets us know at the outset that Joseph's life is essential to the unfolding of God's plan.

NUPTIAL LOVE

The covenant God established with Abraham and his descendants is rightly described as nuptial (see *CCC*, 1611). St. Matthew means to recount the birth and life of Jesus within a nuptial context, because he has come to see Christ as the Bridegroom for whom God has been preparing the people of Israel. Every sign and wonder God performed in the past was a preparation for the coming of the one whose flesh and blood would eternally unite the human family with God in a nuptial relationship, described in sacred Scripture as "the marriage supper of the Lamb" (Revelation 19:9).

Joseph's life quite literally has its origins in God's saving action. His lineage alone assures us that he is "a helper fit" for the woman who bears God's Son (Genesis 2:18). I would go so far as to say that God's saving action is woven into Joseph's very identity. This is why he accepts all that the angel tells him concerning the way in which the child came to be conceived in the womb of the woman to whom he is betrothed: "That which is conceived in her is of the Holy Spirit; she will bear a son, and you shall call his name Jesus, for he will save his people from their sins" (Matthew 1:20–21).

Joseph's willingness to take Mary as his wife enables the outpouring of God's grace to begin healing the rupture caused by sin within the most appropriate situation: married life. Through their union as husband and wife, grace is unleashed in the world. By taking Mary into his home, the grace of God, already present in she who is "full of grace" (Luke 1:28), builds on Joseph's nature. His righteousness grows in her presence and in that of her son. It is precisely God's plan that their relationship as husband and wife become a definitive sign of that which God intended from the beginning: "what no eye has seen, nor ear heard, / nor the heart of man conceived" (1 Corinthians 2:9).

As the "first couple" in this unprecedented event, Joseph and Mary will "be fruitful and multiply, and fill the earth and subdue it" (Genesis 1:28) in an entirely new order. Their mutual, reciprocal, and faithful love will be expressed in the order of grace and sustained by the over-shadowing of the Holy Spirit (see Matthew 1:20). By the time Joseph takes Mary into his home, each of them has learned that God is up to something overwhelmingly difficult to believe (see Matthew 1:20–24; Luke 1:26–35). They know that the union of their lives, centered on Jesus, will extend well beyond the ordinary demands of family life. God is inviting them to fulfill a plan formed long before either of them came to be, a plan that will be carried out by Mary's son:

He chose us in him before the foundation of the world, that we should be holy and blameless before him. He destined us in love to be his sons through Jesus Christ, according to the purpose of his will, to the praise of his glorious grace which he freely bestowed on us in the Beloved. In him we have redemption through his blood, the forgiveness of our trespasses, according to the riches of his grace which he lavished upon us. For he has made known to us in all wisdom and insight the mystery of his will, according to his purpose which he set forth in Christ as a plan for the fulness of time, to unite all things in him, things in heaven and things on earth. (Ephesians 1:4–10)

Joseph and Mary's life does not fit into ordinary human categories. The union of their lives as man and woman, while pointing back to the beginning, also points toward "a new heaven and a new earth" that Mary's son will establish (Revelation 21:1). God has chosen them to play a role in restoring what was lost by sin. More than that, they are part of the kingdom that is yet to be. "The old has passed away, behold, the new has come" (2 Corinthians 5:17).

So from the beginning of Matthew's Gospel we learn that Joseph's life is more than that of Mary's caretaker. While he certainly is that, his relationship with Mary is, by grace, truly and most fittingly nuptial. The love and affection between them mirrors their love for God, for he is fully present with them. This love they fully express, free of the recriminations, selfishness, and urges to control that result from sin. They will see and love in each other what God sees and loves in them. They will "set [their] minds on things that are above," the world that will never end (Colossians 3:2).

This union of their lives in God precludes the need to experience the union of their bodies in conjugal love. What they share with each other through, with, and in the power of the Holy Spirit transcends erotic desire. Their chaste love becomes the means by which each will "glorify

God" in the body (1 Corinthians 6:20). Through the power of the Most High, Mary is joined to the Lord; we call her "the spouse of the Holy Spirit." By taking Mary as his wife, Joseph is likewise joined to the Lord. So by the time they are united in marriage, Joseph and Mary have truly become one in spirit with God. "He who is united to the Lord becomes one spirit with him" (1 Corinthians 6:17).

Their wedded life is not a rejection of marital intercourse but rather a sign of God's kingdom, where men and women "neither marry nor are given in marriage" (Matthew 22:30). Their love as husband and wife is a "purification" of erotic love, free of its entanglement with flesh and the resulting "debasement" of human sexuality.[2] Joseph and Mary give married life and love an eternal horizon: Their life together continually points toward the eternal, to God.

This new and decisive direction will extend to all married couples, albeit in diverse ways. It is Jesus's call to his disciples: They are to lose their lives and deny themselves for him in order that they might preserve and truly discover themselves in him (see Matthew 10:34; 16:25; Luke 17:33). By their willingness to become husband and wife, Joseph and Mary clothe themselves in a love that contains all human categories of love.

> Put on then, as God's chosen ones, holy and beloved, compassion, kindness, lowliness, meekness, and patience, forbearing one another and, if one has a complaint against another, forgiving each other; as the Lord has forgiven you, so you also must forgive. And over all these put on love, which binds everything together in perfect harmony. (Colossians 3:12–14)

A SACRAMENTAL MARRIAGE

Together Joseph and Mary prepare the way that leads to the elevation of marriage as a sacrament. Jesus will grow up in a home free of the disorders caused by original sin. His future descriptions of life in God's kingdom are already apparent in the peace and joy of the home at Nazareth. During a wedding feast in Cana, Jesus will change water into wine, thereby confirming "the goodness of marriage and the proclamation that thenceforth marriage will be an efficacious sign of Christ's presence" (*CCC*, 1613).

The home at Nazareth endures as a school of the communion between man and woman that God intended from the beginning. It can rightly be described as the first "domestic church." For "It is in the bosom of the family that parents are 'by word and example...the first heralds of the faith with regard to their children'" (*CCC*, 1656).[3] By their fidelity to God, Joseph and Mary provide a dynamic "witness of a holy life, and self-denial and active charity" (*CCC*, 1657).[4]

As Jesus grows to manhood, the life of his parents gives witness to the vibrant reciprocity of love of God and neighbor that will become the basis of his preaching. After thirty-some years of being educated in this home, established by his heavenly Father but headed by his earthly one, Jesus's announcement that the "kingdom of God is at hand" is no abstract claim (Mark 1:15). His words resound with an authority never before encountered: "He taught them as one who had authority, and not as the scribes" (Mark 1:22). He speaks from the depths of his lived experience—not only his eternal existence with the Father but also his earthly habitation with Joseph and Mary. Jesus has seen in the love of Joseph and Mary the fruitful obedience that will "fill the earth and subdue it" (Genesis 1:28).

We can also say that Joseph's willingness to take Mary into his home is much more than the proper deed of a "just man," as Matthew describes him (Matthew 1:19). It is the decisive act of a man who understands himself in terms of his relationship with God. Joseph's life has been rooted in an adherence to the commandments, ordinances, and decrees of God, even before an angel visits him in a dream. This enables him to both understand and accept everything the angel tells him.

Joseph awakens from his dream determined to welcome God's plan. He knows that his marriage to Mary is more than one of mere utility or necessity. By the grace of God, Joseph is emboldened to yield the entirety of his life to the woman whose son "will save his people from their sins" (Matthew 1:21). Like Adam awakening from the deep sleep God cast upon him to find Eve by his side, "bone of my bones and flesh of my flesh" (Genesis 2:23), Joseph awakens and sees in Mary the woman who will complete his life in the most unexpected and unprecedented way.

Matthew's seemingly short account of the spousal relationship of Joseph and Mary asserts that their union was initiated by God. "Joseph, son of David, do not fear to take Mary your wife," the angel said to Joseph (Matthew 1:20). This is truly God speaking, for "the angels are *servants* and messengers of God. Because they 'always behold the face of my Father who is in heaven' they are the 'mighty ones who do his word, hearkening to the voice of his word'" (*CCC*, 329).[5]

Joseph, as the husband of Mary, is a tangible and lasting sign of our destiny, for "The entire Christian life bears the mark of the spousal love of Christ and the Church" (*CCC*, 1617). We are destined to be forever wedded to one another in God. Joseph is faithful to Mary—loving, honoring, respecting, and protecting her all the days of his life—just as God is faithful to the Church.

God has given St. Joseph to the Church as a fitting example for all Christian husbands to follow: "Husbands, love your wives, as Christ loved the Church and gave himself up for her" (Ephesians 5:25). For Mary, Joseph renounces himself and his plans. He takes upon himself the responsibility for her child—providing a home, teaching Jesus to pray, instructing him in a trade, and preparing him for his public ministry. Joseph receives the grace to do so—not in the abstract—but in the flesh and blood of Mary's son, who perfects Joseph's human love and strengthens him to live the totality of his vocation.

At the dawn of Christianity, married life and love are given new "breadth and length and height and depth" (Ephesians 3:18). Joseph and Mary, as husband and wife, become an icon of Christian marriage, which "in its turn" will be "an efficacious sign, the sacrament of Christ and the Church" (*CCC*, 1617). They are an incarnate expression of human communion, which expresses the very life of God. They are wedded not simply to provide a fitting home for the child; they are wedded so that men and women can know what it means to be wedded to God.

Together Joseph and Mary espouse the new covenant of God's love. They share this life of love with one another as a fitting sign of the love that will express itself on the altar of the cross.

CHAPTER TWO

THE FATHER OF JESUS

Do you not believe that I am in the Father and the Father is in me? The words that I say to you I do not speak on my own authority; but the Father who dwells in me does his works. Believe me that I am in the Father and the Father is in me; or else believe me for the sake of the works themselves.

Truly, truly, I say to you, he who believes in me will also do the works that I do; and greater works than these will he do, because I go to the Father. (John 14:10–12)

WHILE RETURNING HOME FROM ONE of their yearly visits to Jerusalem, Joseph and Mary discover that Jesus is not with them (see Luke 2:44). Going back to the city, they find the boy after a three-day search, "sitting among the teachers, listening to them and asking them questions" (2:46). Astonished at what they see, Mary asks Jesus why he has done what he has. She tells him, "Your father and I have been looking for you anxiously" (2:48).

By expressing her maternal concern in this way, Mary establishes the distinctive characteristic of Joseph's vocation. He is not only her spouse but also a father to Jesus in every way a child needs one.

The astounding scene offers a glimpse of the relationship between Jesus and his earthly father. It also provides an occasion for the revelation of Jesus's divine nature. God's plan is to usher in the revelation, through his Son, that he is Father as no one is father. He "is the first origin of everything and transcendent authority; and…he is at the same time goodness and loving care for all his children" (*CCC*, 239).[6] "Call no man your father on earth," Jesus will later say, "for you have one Father, who is in heaven" (Matthew 23:9).

Luke here gives us a window into the life at Nazareth by drawing our attention away from Joseph and Mary's search and highlighting instead the unexpected depth of knowledge of their twelve-year-old son (Luke 2:47). That a young man from a small, impoverished, rural town can competently engage with men of learning and experience is certainly surreal. The boy wonder is the focus here; likewise he was the focus of Joseph's life. While all parents are called to be the "first representatives of God" (*CCC*, 239)[7] for their children, God filled Joseph's home in more than a representative manner.

It was Joseph's responsibility to educate his son about the precepts of the Law: "And these words which I command you…you shall teach… diligently to your children" (Deuteronomy 6:6). What did this mean for Joseph, as his son had written the precepts in communion with the Father? How did he teach prayer to one who was already bound to the Father in the depth to which all prayer aspires?

It's reasonable to conclude that the comfort Jesus exhibits in the Temple indicates the comfort he must have found when discussing spiritual matters in the home at Nazareth. The relative ease with which Jesus stays behind in Jerusalem likewise flows from the freedom cultivated in his family home. At the start of their return to Nazareth, neither Joseph nor Mary seems concerned that Jesus is not with them. They continue on their way for a full day, assuming that he is part of the caravan. Only then do they begin to look for him among relatives and friends (see Luke 2:44). They return to Jerusalem after their search has failed.

While we know the anxiety of the three-day search, we know little of where they look and why. Perhaps they come back to the Temple as a last resort, hoping their desperate prayers for God's assistance will be heard. God, however, has something more in mind than quieting their fears and answering their prayers. He broadens their understanding of the child who "will reign over the house of Jacob for ever" (Luke 1:33).

In this moment of discovery, Joseph and Mary learn a new facet of Jesus's life, namely its connection with the Temple. Jesus's response to Mary is not the disrespectful retort of a teenage boy but the heartfelt reply of a young man who knows who he is. The confidence with which Jesus speaks these words to Mary, as confusing as they are (Luke 2:50), demonstrate that his parents' lives, too, are centered on being "in my Father's house" (Luke 2:49). He expects them to understand, because he sees his life reflected in theirs.

God the Father's work encompasses the home in Nazareth. "The obedience of Christ in the daily routine of his hidden life was already inaugurating his work of restoring what the disobedience of Adam had destroyed" (*CCC*, 532).[8] Thus Jesus returns to Nazareth with Joseph and Mary, recognizing that their responsibility in raising him is also inextricably bound with the Father. The wisdom, stature, and favor in which Jesus will advance are a direct fruit of the obedience to his parents that will distinguish the next eighteen years of his life (Luke 2:52). This obedience "was the temporal image of his filial obedience to his Father in heaven" (*CCC*, 532).

What isn't recounted about Joseph in the infancy narratives is nonetheless told through the actions, teachings, and disposition of Jesus during his public ministry. As his proclamation of the kingdom of God unfolds, we learn valuable insights about Jesus's course of study under Joseph's tutelage. As Pope Paul VI reminded us, "The home of Nazareth is the school where we begin to understand the life of Jesus—the school of the Gospel" (*CCC*, 533).⁹

FEMALE FRIENDS

One of the most important lessons fathers must teach their sons is proper conduct toward women. In this regard, Jesus was extremely fortunate. The person most responsible for his growth to manhood exhibited love, respect, and concern for Mary. Joseph's devotion to his wife was not predicated on the revelation in his dream but upon the woman he had come to know and had betrothed to himself. Learning the truth of Mary's condition only strengthened Joseph's love for her and gave that love a decisively new direction.

Jesus's respect for women was noteworthy. We see it reflected in the way he welcomed women as valued friends (see Luke 10:38–42; John 11:1–4), accepted them into the company of his followers (Luke 8:1–3), praised their faith (Mark 7:24–30), made himself available to them (John 4:7–42), and responded in mercy to their sinfulness (John 8:1–11).

A principal example of Jesus's friendships with women is that with Martha and Mary. In Luke's account we learn that each sister had a distinctive bond with Jesus. Mary recognized Jesus to be a holy man. His words resonated with such genuineness that she was content to sit at his feet and listen (Luke 10:39). Jesus's words were comforting, and Mary would in turn comfort Jesus by anointing his feet with aromatic nard and drying them with her hair (John 12:3). Mary was at ease in Jesus's presence, readily putting aside household chores to learn from her friend, who knew the deepest desires of her heart.

Jesus loved to have Mary spend time with him in this way. Perhaps the home at Bethany mirrored that at Nazareth, where he, Mary, and Joseph would sit and listen to one another. Surely they reflected on the amazing events of Jesus's life. By the time he was able to ask questions, his mother already held in her heart a precious treasury of memories (see Luke 2:19). As parents are fond of recounting the story of their child's life, Joseph and Mary would have done the same. Perhaps Jesus shared some of this story with his friends Mary, Martha, and their brother, Lazarus. Certainly he could insightfully and confidently share the great goodness of the Lord with the family in Bethany.

Martha, although initially "anxious and troubled about many things" (Luke 10:41), eventually came to see her friend Jesus from the same perspective as did St. Peter. She was able to look beyond the responsibilities and cares of the home to the truth that Jesus is "the Christ, the Son of God, he who is coming into the world" (John 11:27). Martha moved from being comfortable enough to ask Jesus for Mary's help to being comfortable with his absence at the death of her brother (John 11:17). She was confident that God would give Jesus whatever he asked. While Mary remained at home grieving, Martha went out to meet Jesus (John 11:20).

Martha and Jesus meet just outside of town, and there we learn how Martha has come to choose "the good portion" (Luke 10:42). This is reflected in her faith-filled words to a man who has become more than a friend: "Lord, if you had been here, my brother would not have died. And even now I know that whatever you ask from God, God will give you" (John 11:21–22).

Martha knows that her brother will rise at the resurrection on the last day. Her testimony allows Jesus to openly share the truth of his being the "resurrection and the life" (John 11:25). These words in turn prepare his disciples for the work Jesus has come to accomplish, that they, too, might believe (see John 11:15).

Martha is not content to keep Jesus for herself. She goes home in order to bring Mary to their friend. Mary falls at Jesus's feet, lamenting the fact that he was not with them when Lazarus died. Jesus asks to be taken to Lazarus's tomb. As we move with them toward the place where Lazarus has been buried, we learn just how much Jesus loves them. He openly weeps at the loss of his friend (see John 11:35).

GRATEFUL FOLLOWERS

Martha and Mary were not the only women to whom Jesus opened his life. Accompanying him and the twelve were "Mary, called Magdalene... Joanna the wife of Chuza, Herod's steward, and Susanna, and many others, who provided for them out of their means" (Luke 8:2–3). Some of these had been cured of evil spirits and infirmities. They were not sent back to their homes, as were many men whom Jesus healed (see Matthew 9:6–7; Mark 8:26; Luke 8:39). Perhaps the women would have been exposed to scrutiny, judgment, and shame. Jesus showed the same loving discretion that Joseph had shown toward Mary when he discovered her pregnancy (Matthew 1:19).

Such discretion is assuredly the case with the woman caught in adultery (see John 8:3–11). Rather than become entangled in a discussion about the accusations being made, Jesus quietly traces his finger in the sand, and then challenges the righteousness of the accusers: "Let him who is without sin among you be the first to throw a stone at her" (John 8:7). The men leave "one by one, beginning with the eldest." There is now no one there to condemn her, and neither will Jesus.

Jesus's actions not only save the woman's life but also reorient it. Alone with her now, he is able to speak to her directly: "Do not sin again" (John 8:11).

This woman and many like her find their true place only within the company of Jesus's followers. A growing number of them travel from village to village with Jesus as he proclaims the Good News of God's kingdom (see Mark 15:40–41).

All four Gospels make it abundantly clear that Jesus's message is for women as well as men. His words and actions perfectly reveal the truth that "God shows no partiality" (Acts 10:34). Jesus came to call all sinners to repentance, whoever they might be and wherever they might be found (Luke 5:32). He moves throughout Galilee and Judea, including places not inhabited by the children of the house of Israel.

He ventures to places like Samaria, where a Jew was not expected to go. There, in a town called Sychar, Jesus sits down at Jacob's well, while his disciples go into town to buy food (see John 4:5–8). In the middle of the day, a Samaritan woman comes to the well, and this intriguing Jewish man engages her in a spirited conversation. What begins with a simple request for a drink of water will forever change this woman's life and the lives of the people in her village (John 4:42).

Jesus shows once again that his righteousness is not revealed in condemning others but in offering them the chance of "eternal life" (John 4:14). At the end of their conversation, the woman hurries back to town, unafraid of what others may think of her. Like Martha, she cannot keep Jesus to herself but is compelled to invite others to come and meet the man who "told me all that I ever did" (John 4:39). Jesus ends up staying in Sychar for two days, so that all the people in the town might draw "living water" from him (John 4:10).

As Jesus went about healing the sick, raising the dead, and casting out demons, he regularly encountered men and women of remarkable faith. He singled out one woman as "a daughter of Abraham" (Luke 13:16). He commended a Canaanite: "O woman, great is your faith!" and healed her daughter from the torments of a demon (Matthew 15:21–28).

The way in which Jesus interacted with women is a profound testimony to the love of the Father and the example of his earthly father. St. Joseph was a model of masculinity, and his strength was rooted in thoughtful care and genuine respect. His unwillingness to expose Mary to shame reveals the depth of his character, as does his attentive care of Mary at the time of Christ's birth. Joseph is, with Mary, a living witness to the light that will reveal to the nations God's saving power (Luke 2:32).

Jesus taught that the measure with which we measure will be the measure used toward us (Matthew 7:2). Joseph poured out his life for God, and that life overflowed with God's goodness.

The Word that was with the Father in the beginning (see John 1:1) needed a human voice to speak the truth of God's love to a world disordered by sin. Therefore God chose and prepared the most fitting vessel by which his Son might be born of flesh and blood. He also chose with great care the man perfectly suited for the rearing of his Son. Joseph showed through his care of Jesus what being a father truly means. Jesus in turn would show the world the Father.

CHAPTER THREE

MAN OF OBEDIENCE

Sacrifice and offering you do not desire;
  but you have given me an open ear.
Burnt offering and sin offering
  you have not required.
Then I said, "Behold, I come;
  in the roll of the book it is written of me;
I delight to do your will, O my God,
  your law is within my heart." (Psalm 40:6–8)

THE VIRTUE OF OBEDIENCE CAN be difficult to understand today. Ours is a culture in which self-determination has been carried to destructive extremes.

Blessed are those who know the truth of God's Word: Such is St. Joseph. As soon as we meet him at the beginning of Matthew's Gospel, he pushes back any notion of obedience as a necessary evil for the sustenance of certain social structures.

Joseph is a righteous man. Prior to Jesus's coming, righteousness essentially referred to one's moral character, wholly determined by one's adherence to everything Moses set before the people in the wilderness:

I am the LORD your God....
You shall have no other gods before me.
...You shall not take the name of the LORD your God in vain....

Observe the Sabbath day, to keep it holy.…
Honor your father and your mother.…
You shall not kill.
Neither shall you commit adultery.
Neither shall you steal.
Neither shall you bear false witness against your neighbor.
Neither shall you covet your neighbor's wife; and you shall not desire your neighbor's house, his field, or his manservant, or his maidservant, his ox, or his donkey, or anything that is your neighbor's. (Deuteronomy 5:6, 7, 11, 12, 16, 17–21).

Thus we know that Joseph's distinguishing characteristic presented at the beginning of Matthew's Gospel is his lived obedience to the Law.

A LEGAL DILEMMA

Just as in Luke's Gospel, Matthew deliberately highlights in the story of Jesus's birth the perspective of individuals acting according to God's will—the "handmaid of the Lord" and the man who "did as the angel of the Lord commanded him" (Luke 1:38; Matthew 1:24). Each author presents the reader with a fundamental transformation from the old understanding of obedience to the new. By accepting God's plan, both Mary and Joseph are freed from the Pharisaical legalism that Jesus will later condemn (see Luke 14:1–5). Their yes is not a rejection of all that the Law and the prophets demand, but a sign of its fulfillment.

Previous to the coming of Christ, observance of the Law was the means by which a person could experience the fulfillment of all the promises of God's covenant with his people:

God said to Abraham, "…You shall keep my covenant, you and your descendants after you throughout their generations. This is my covenant, which you shall keep, between me and you and your descendants after you." (Genesis 17:9, 10)

The LORD called to [Moses] out of the mountain, saying, "...Now therefore, if you will obey my voice and keep my covenant, you shall be my own possession among all peoples; for all the earth is mine, and you shall be to me a kingdom of priests and a holy nation. These are the words which you shall speak to the children of Israel." (Exodus 19:3, 5–6)

The mother of seven sons in the second book of Maccabees exhorted them to be faithful to the Law as they faced martyrdom: "The Creator of the world, who shaped the beginning of man and devised the origin of all things, will in his mercy give life and breath back to you again, since you now forget yourselves for the sake of his laws" (2 Maccabees 7:23).

Obedience served to strengthen the community and preserve it from distress. Although this virtue acquired more personal implications after the time of Israel's exile, love of God was expressed almost entirely through one's love of the Law. Joseph certainly believed that "the ordinances of the LORD are true, / and righteous altogether" (Psalm19:9). Thus God could entrust the Holy Family to him.

Before the angel spoke to him in a dream, Joseph's experience of God came almost entirely through his faithful observance of the Law. Like other faithful members of his people, he believed in the Law in a way similar to the way Christians believe in Christ. Observance of the Law gave him access to God.

Thus we can understand Joseph's struggle when he learns of Mary's pregnancy (Matthew 1:19). He knows full well what the Law requires:

If there is a betrothed virgin, and a man meets her in the city and lies with her, then you shall bring them both out to the gate of that city, and you shall stone them to death with stones…; so you shall purge the evil from the midst of you. (Deuteronomy 22:23–24)

But Joseph also cares deeply for the woman and hesitates to "put her to shame" (Matthew 1:19), much less put her to death. The Law, which prior to this moment governed every aspect of his life, suddenly becomes a burden. His decision to quietly divorce Mary is an attempt to be respectful toward her and toward the Law.

Trying to determine the right way through this unexpected turn of events is the first spiritual trial Joseph faces on account of the woman and her child. Here he begins to learn obedience through suffering (see Hebrews 5:8). In fact, as the story of Jesus's birth unfolds, obedience to the Father will repeatedly require sacrifice on Joseph's part.

The words the angel speaks to Joseph in his dream initiate a radical transformation in his concept of obedience. While *obedience* has its origins in a word meaning "to hear," implying a readiness to listen and to act, observance of the Law did not require a personal message from the voice of God. People acted on what had been spoken through Moses and the prophets; they trusted the authority of those who handed on and interpreted God's Word. The Law was the means by which God's people had contact with him, and obedience was a way of conveying one's belief that God had indeed spoken "of old to our fathers by the prophets" (Hebrews 1:1).

When Joseph awakens from his dream, his perspective has changed. The truth about Mary's pregnancy and the description of her child make his obedience unreservedly personal. Joseph's orientation shifts decisively: His relationship with God will no longer be centered upon the Law but on Mary and her child. While Joseph will continue to do all that the Law requires (see Luke 2:22–23, for example), this will not be the primary means by which he loves God and experiences God's love. Like Jacob his ancestor, Joseph awakens from his dream knowing God in a previously unimagined way. He is confident that taking Mary and Jesus into his abode is "the gate of heaven" (Genesis 28:17).

This, of course, will change the whole of Joseph's life. The son he's raising is the fulfillment of "the law and the prophets" (Matthew 5:17), the fulfillment of all God's promises. Obedience to the Father opens Joseph's life to the very "righteousness of God" (2 Corinthians 5:21), for which each one of us has been created.

As life with Mary and Jesus unfolds, Joseph will gain an ever-deepening awareness that obedience to God is an experience of true human freedom. By accepting God's plan, Joseph welcomes grace into his life. He could never lay claim to this grace; rather he receives it as the gift it is.

In obeying God, Joseph becomes the man he is truly meant to be. Mary and Jesus will be the mirrors that reflect the image Joseph has of God. Indeed, through them he comes to see God and others and all of reality in new ways.

In the tangible conditions of the daily life of the Holy Family, Joseph experiences the presence of God and the fulfillment of his promises. This "new way" upon which Joseph embarks after awakening from his dream is the pathway that leads to the everlasting life that Jesus will later describe (see Luke 18:18–23). In welcoming Mary into his home, Joseph "leaves his father and mother and clings to his wife" (Genesis 2:24). He thus is the first to inherit Christ's promise: "Everyone who has left houses or brothers or sisters or father or mother or children or lands, for my name's sake, will receive a hundredfold, and inherit eternal life" (Matthew 19:29).

The transformation that takes place in the life of Joseph will greatly influence Mary's child during the course of his growth to manhood.

Jesus is the ultimate "wise son [who] hears his father's instruction" (Proverbs 13:1). He will subject the formative years of his life to this humble man, for this is the will of the Father in heaven.

THE WAY TO FREEDOM

Jesus's obedience is clear from the start of his public ministry (see Matthew 4:1–11; Luke 4:1–13). He withstands the temptation of Satan to make bread out of stone by the "word that proceeds from the mouth of God," the word by which men and women are ultimately sustained (Matthew 4:4). Satan departs from Jesus "until an opportune time" (Luke 4:13).

Satan is always a failure in the face of Jesus's steadfast obedience to the Father. Demons must submit to Jesus's authority (see Mark 1:23–26; 5:2–13). He can command them because he speaks on behalf of the Father. The unclean spirits know that Jesus's words are not his own; his words resonate with the dynamism with which "all things…visible and invisible" (Colossians 1:16) came into existence. The Word that was with the Father in the beginning (see John 1:1) is now present in the world as a man. No one will take Jesus's life from him—not Judas, the crowds, or even Pilate. Jesus alone has the power to lay down his life.

The obedience Jesus displayed in the home at Nazareth is the "gate" by which the King of Glory reveals himself.

> Lift up your heads, O gates!
>   and be lifted up, O ancient doors!
>   that the King of glory may come in.
> Who is the King of glory?
>   The LORD, strong and mighty,
>   the LORD, mighty in battle!
> Lift up your heads, O gates!

and be lifted up, O ancient doors!
that the King of glory may come in.
Who is this King of glory?
The LORD of hosts,
he is the King of glory! (Psalm 24:7–10)

Jesus, in submitting to Joseph and Mary, submitted his will to his heavenly Father:

Honor your father and your mother, that your days may be long in the land which the LORD your God gives you. (Exodus 20:12)

Every one of you shall revere his mother and his father...; I am the LORD your God. (Leviticus 19:3)

Jesus's model of obedience, through which the many will be made righteous (see Romans 5:19), is the model for all Christ's followers. The redemption Christ won for us only comes about through the same lived obedience that characterized Jesus's life and was definitively expressed by his death on the cross. We are called to imitate Christ, to live just as he lived, even to the point of laying down our lives:

This is my commandment, that you love one another as I have loved you. Greater love has no man than this, that a man lay down his life for his friends. You are my friends if you do what I command you. No longer do I call you servants, for the servant does not know what his master is doing; but I have called you friends, for all that I have heard from my Father I have made known to you. You did not choose me, but I chose you and appointed you that you should go and bear fruit and that your fruit should abide; so that whatever you ask the

Father in my name, he may give it to you. This I command you, to love one another. (John 15:12–17).

We are called to be women and men who obediently take up our crosses (see Matthew 10:38). They are our participation in the cross of our Lord Jesus Christ, "by which the world has been crucified to [us], and [we] to the world" (Galatians 6:14). Joseph's life teaches us to do just that: We are to lose ourselves for the sake of the Gospel (see Mark 8:34–38).

Joseph is a worthy disciple of his son: He knows that human freedom comes only by carrying out the Father's will. His free gift of his life in obedience to the Father foretells Jesus's own.

Christ "communicated to his disciples the gift of royal freedom, so that they might 'by the self-abnegation of a holy life, overcome the reign of sin in themselves'" (CCC, 908).[10] The more good we do, the freer we become. Joseph's life is an example of complete and free submission to the Father's will. The man who lived with Jesus longer than any other man shows us obedience to the Father within the real circumstances of daily human life. He reminds us that even the most arduous times can be sources of overwhelming grace, because the curse of death has been transformed into a blessing by the suffering and death of Christ (see CCC, 1009; Romans 5:19–21).

When Joseph awakens from his dream, Mary and Jesus in a real sense are his only law. Let's ask St. Joseph's help in awakening us to the truth of our belonging to Christ and being in Christ. For through our obedience to Christ, we have redemption and the forgiveness of our sins. When, like Joseph, we willingly lay down our lives for Christ, we can "overcome the reign of sin" and be truly righteous.

We all have a part to play in the accomplishment of the plan of God, "on earth as it is in heaven" (Matthew 6:10). That particular role comes from God. Like Joseph, let us be attentive to the voice of God: "O that today you would listen to his voice!" (Psalm 95:7). And let us obey:

> To obey is better than sacrifice,
>   and to listen than the fat of rams. (1 Samuel 15:22)

CHAPTER FOUR

MAN OF FAITH

"Great is the mystery of the faith!" The Church professes this mystery in the Apostles' Creed (*Part One*) and celebrates it in the sacramental liturgy (*Part Two*), so that the life of the faithful may be conformed to Christ in the Holy Spirit to the glory of God the Father (*Part Three*). This mystery, then, requires that the faithful believe in it, that they celebrate it, and that they live it in a vital and personal relationship with the living and true God. (*CCC*, 2558)

THE BIRTH OF JESUS COMES about because of the extraordinary faith and determined obedience of his mother Mary—her *fiat*, "Let it be to me according to your word" (Luke 1:38). Mary has conceived by the power of the Holy Spirit, that God might literally be with his people through the flesh and blood of her son:

And behold, you will conceive in your womb and bear a son, and you shall call his name Jesus.
He will be great, and will be called the Son of the Most High; and the Lord God will give to him the throne of his father David,
and he will reign over the house of Jacob for ever; and of his kingdom there will be no end."
And Mary said to the angel, "How can this be, since I have no husband?" And the angel said to her,
"The Holy Spirit will come upon you,

and the power of the Most High will overshadow you;
therefore the child to be born will be called holy,
the Son of God." (Luke 1:31–35)

Joseph is the man of faith whom God calls to participate intimately in
this pivotal phase of his plan of salvation. Joseph is a member of God's
people whose lineage is inextricably linked with the entire history of
Israel: Abraham, Isaac, Jacob, Judah, and even the great King David are
in his family line (see Matthew 1:1–6; Luke 3:23–38). As an upright
Jew, Joseph knew that there could be no savior but God:

> "You are my witnesses," says the Lord,
> "and my servant whom I have chosen,
> that you may know and believe me
> and understand that I am He.
> Before me no god was formed,
> nor shall there be any after me.
> I, I am the Lord,
> and besides me there is no savior.
> I declared and saved and proclaimed,
> when there was no strange god among you;
> and you are my witnesses," says the Lord.
> "I am God, and also henceforth I am He;
> there is none who can deliver from my hand;
> I work and who can hinder it?" (Isaiah 43:10–13)

This is a man who trusts God's promises and has lived in obedience to
his commandments.

Touched by an Angel

In order to continue being a man of faith, Joseph must now accept the
astonishing words of an angel:

Joseph, son of David, do not fear to take Mary your wife, for that which is conceived in her is of the Holy Spirit; she will bear a son, and you shall call his name Jesus, for he will save his people from their sins. (Matthew 1:20–21)

This message lies beyond the scope of Joseph's intellection. Only a careful examination of the Scriptures could lead anyone to conclude that God would save his people by becoming one with them. This moment of Christian faith in Matthew's Gospel comes to a man whom God has taken the initiative to lead in an entirely new way.

The message centers on the child conceived in Mary. Joseph must accept the fact that Jesus is indeed the promised and long-awaited Savior. Taking such a step requires faith, and Joseph takes it. His dream punctuates the vitality of his faith, which he will express through his comprehensive commitment to Jesus.

Joseph's willingness to welcome Mary into his home and his life expresses Christian faith perfectly. It is not a faith directed so much at a message, creed, or moral code as it is directed to the human life Mary carries within her. Joseph awakens from the dream knowing, however indistinctly, God's word of salvation: "And the Word became flesh and dwelt among us, full of grace and truth; we have beheld his glory, glory as of the only-begotten Son from the Father" (John 1:14).

The visitation of the angel changes Joseph's conception of revelation. He, neither a prophet nor a king nor an elder of Israel, has received a word of great moment from God. God has elected a definitive and decisively new way to draw near to men and women: a child, Mary's child. Through the incarnation of his eternal Word, God establishes a communion between himself and the world. This communion will save us from the solitude, isolation, and "death of the soul" that came about as a result of original sin (*CCC*, 403). By accepting the fact that Mary's child is indeed the Son of God, Joseph's life opens to the "love of the Father in the Spirit" that is mediated through communion with Christ (*CCC*, 426).[11]

Joseph willingly yields to the plan of God because it touches something deep within his heart. His innate hunger for the eternal has been awakened. It is now drawn toward the greatest sign and wonder ever worked by God, and here it will be rooted. All that Joseph has hoped for and believed up to this point is given flesh and blood in Mary's son. Faith becomes as tangible for Joseph as the child he will raise. Joseph will not build his life on his own works in accordance with the Law but on God's work, which means believing in the one he has sent (see John 6:28–29). Joseph will become a living embodiment of what it means to commit oneself entirely to God's Word, whom he will see and hear and touch with his hands (see 1 John 1:1).

Joseph's visit with the angel emphasizes for us the fact that God always takes the first step in human faith. All hearts naturally long for the eternal, and only God can answer this longing. By reaching out to us in Christ, God offers us the satisfaction of our hearts' desire. When we accept in truth the words of the angel, we gain with Joseph "the assurance of things hoped for, the conviction of things not seen" (Hebrews 11:1).

We also gain with Joseph a new concept of God. Since Mary's child has been conceived through the power of the Holy Spirit and is the "Son of the Most High," we can no longer think of God as being solitary and alone and distant. The Mystery responsible for creating all things reveals himself to Joseph in terms of relationship. Joseph awakens to the truth of "the mystery of the Holy Trinity, [which] is the central mystery of Christian faith and life" (*CCC*, 234).

WALKING BY FAITH

By submitting the entirety of their lives to God, Mary and Joseph become the "first couple," as it were, of New Testament faith. The trust that God required of Israel (see Genesis 15:6; Exodus 14:31; Numbers 14:11) is now more explicitly defined because the incarnate Word of God is now wed to salvation history. Jesus is the new and distinctive star by which God's people will order their lives. Faith in God is, now and forever, faith in Jesus. As Joseph and Mary raise this child, each will come to know in a deeper way the Father who sent him. "He who has seen me has seen the Father," Jesus will later tell Philip (John 14:9), and certainly his parents saw a lot of him!

Joseph will express his trust and his willing surrender to God in his assent to the words and actions of Jesus. God is not an idea or an abstraction; he has chosen to make himself known in the most remarkable way. Joseph will believe the angel's words, and this belief will sustain him in the face of challenging demands and arduous conditions.

The first of these challenges is the actual conditions of Jesus's birth. Joseph brings his very pregnant wife to the town of his heritage in order to participate in an enrollment ordered by Caesar Augustus. Amid the crowds he must find a room where the child can be born. He looks to God in the dilemma of a packed inn. And the Lamb of God is born in what is perhaps the most suitable of all places: "And she gave birth to her first-born son and wrapped him in swaddling cloths, and laid him in a manger" (Luke 2:7).

Joseph probably did not know the significance of the Bread of Life's birth in a manger in Bethlehem, a name that means "house of bread." Yet the shepherds confirm his drive to move toward God as they recount what was spoken to them by the angel in the field:

> Be not afraid; for behold, I bring you good news of a great joy which will come to all the people; for to you is born this day

in the city of David a Savior, who is Christ the Lord. And this will be a sign for you: you will find a baby wrapped in swaddling cloths and lying in a manger. (Luke 2:10–12)

What a consolation this message must be to a man whose life has fundamentally changed because of the words of an angel. I think the haste of the shepherds to see the child mirrors well the haste Joseph demonstrated when he awoke from his dream to undertake all that the angel asked of him: "He did as the angel of the Lord commanded him; he took his wife" (Matthew 1:24).

Sometime after the shepherds leave, the Magi visit, bringing their gifts for the king. Following their departure, Joseph once again has the opportunity to demonstrate the determination with which he looks to God and has set his life upon him. An angel appears in a dream to tell him, "Rise, take the child and his mother, and flee to Egypt, and remain there till I tell you" (Matthew 2:13). There is no reluctance to act or any doubt about what is at stake. "He rose and took the child and his mother by night, and departed to Egypt" (Matthew 2:14). With the security that comes from trusting God completely, he journeys with his young family to a foreign country that holds painful memories for the people of Israel. "This was to fulfil what the Lord had spoken by the prophet, 'Out of Egypt have I called my son'" (Matthew 2:15).

The conditions under which they flee are unthinkable: "Herod is about to search for the child, to destroy him" (Matthew 2:13b). Indeed, Herod will kill all the male children two years of age and younger in an effort to get rid of the future king (see Matthew 2:16). The life of the child Jesus, already a continuing source of wonder and amazement (see Luke 2:33), is being turned upside down. Joseph arrives in Egypt an alien, but fortunately with a trade. This no doubt makes it possible for him to provide shelter and safety for Mary and her precious child until such time as God calls his son (see Matthew 2:15).

In all these early events in the life of Jesus, the angel never revealed the way in which Jesus was to save his people from their sins. No details were given concerning the unfolding of his life. Joseph and Mary raise Jesus without the benefit of the larger picture. While Joseph's life is sometimes punctuated by angelic visitations, these are always concerned with the immediate moment. Joseph repeatedly assents to what is asked of him with a confidence that's rooted in his initial surrender. Joseph "puts his hands to the plow and [never] looks back." Thus, he "is fit for the kingdom of God" (Luke 9:62). He repeatedly sets out in hope because of his trust in the One who called him.

HOUSEHOLD OF FAITH

As mentioned above, Joseph's willingness to surrender to God changes the whole of his existence and transforms his concept and experience of God. His faith is far more than an acceptance of truths, however well articulated. His faith is fundamentally a vibrant expression of his willingness to give himself to God and of God's willingness to give himself to Joseph. In this reciprocal giving Joseph is being transformed into the person God created him to be. Joseph's faith is his life.

The moment we, like Joseph, accept Jesus as the real and only means by which this reciprocal giving can occur, we also begin to appropriate "the mystery of [God's] will" (Ephesians 1:9). We receive the Spirit of love in order to enter the communion of life and love that God wills between himself and humanity.

Joseph is not alone in responding to God's initiatives. His faith is lived and expressed in community with Mary; they are co-believers. Their individual responses are wedded together in a union of life, an expression of belief that transcends the personal. Together they are the first to be nourished and cherished by Christ, even as they nourish and cherish him. They are the original "we" of the Christian community, whom St. Paul will later characterize as "members of [Christ's] body" (Ephesians 5:30).

The beginning of St. Matthew's Gospel accentuates for us the fact that Jesus is both the object of Christian faith and the sole mediator of revelation. God has chosen to make himself known through the child conceived by the power of the Holy Spirit. Joseph already has a sense that the Father has given everything to the child of Mary's womb (Matthew 11:27). He freely accepts having his life "drawn" by this child.

Joseph's faith perfectly illustrates what St. Augustine will later explain:

> It is not by external proclamation of law and doctrine, but by a powerful action which is interior and hidden, wonderful and indescribable, that God becomes the author in human hearts not only of genuine revelations but also of decisions of the will that are in conformity with the good.[12]

God entrusted to St. Joseph the one to whom all the articles of faith point. By welcoming Jesus, Joseph received "the 'Sacred deposit' of the faith" (*CCC*, 84)[13] in the way God intends for each of us. The man Jesus is the conclusive way to God; he is the truth, the meaning, and the purpose of being human; he is the Life who will never let us down.

God reaches toward us. He wants us to know and accept the fact that *he* believes in *us*. "I call you by your name" (Isaiah 45:4). St. Joseph learned this from God's Son. He and Jesus earnestly want us to learn the same.

CHAPTER FIVE

MAN OF HOPE

Hope is the theological virtue by which we desire the kingdom of heaven and eternal life as our happiness, placing our trust in Christ's promises and relying not on our own strength, but on the help of the grace of the Holy Spirit. "Let us hold fast the confession of our hope without wavering, for he who promised is faithful." "The Holy Spirit...he poured out upon us richly through Jesus Christ our Savior, so that we might be justified by his grace and become heirs in hope of eternal life." (*CCC*, 1817)[14]

F OR ST. JOSEPH AND THE whole people of Israel, Abraham was the father and foundation of their hope in God. Confidence, security, trust, expectancy, blessings, and mercy were expressions that grew out of "the *hope of Abraham*, who was blessed abundantly by the promises of God fulfilled in Isaac" (*CCC*, 1819).

This initial sense of hope guided Joseph's life as a faithful member of God's chosen people. Rooted in the historical test of Abraham's willingness to sacrifice his son, it would be directed toward the ever-broadening horizon of the Church's mission. Faithfulness was the bond uniting the past and the future. Thankfulness for the works of God opened Joseph to what Jesus will later promise Nathanael, seeing "greater things than these" (John 1:50).

LIVING HOPE

Joseph's sense of hope is more than simply optimism or a kind of zealous enthusiasm; it is far greater than human sentiment or a self-generated outlook about what might be. The hope that guides Joseph's life is founded in faith and obedience to the laws of God. While this in no way leads Joseph to expect *how* God will act on behalf of his people, it makes him receptive to all manifestations of God's love.

Joseph's dream is such a manifestation—and an exceptional one. God's words, spoken by the angel, respond to the hope of Joseph and his people for true freedom. Jesus will rescue them from their actual bondage: He "will save his people from their sins" (Matthew 1:21). At the same time these words open Joseph's life to an even greater hope, to "desire, and with steadfast trust await from God, eternal life" (*CCC*, 1843).

What had prior to this encounter been a conviction that God would dwell forever with his people has become for Joseph a historical fact. Past, present, and future are all astonishingly woven together in these words about the child conceived in Mary's womb. This boy, an unimaginable manifestation of God's commitment to his people, is in himself hope in its truest sense. Joseph is privileged to be one of the first to experience, welcome, and protect Christian hope.

Hope now has a name, a mother, a family, and a history. In the person of Jesus, hope is truly alive and real—more so than anything Joseph has ever before experienced. Joseph thus reaps from his dream an expanded confidence in and conviction about God's love for his people. His hope, grounded in Mary's child, points to "things not seen" (Hebrews 11:1).

Joseph's life becomes an outstanding example of what it means to live with the tension between the salvation this child represents and the experiences of present conditions and circumstances. Scripture makes it quite clear that Joseph's sense of hope will in no way preserve him from the demanding conditions of real life. Instead it will determine his stance toward whatever happens. Joseph has the assurance of knowing that discouragement, frustration, abandonment, and even suffering cannot define his life or his relationship with God:

> The virtue of hope responds to the aspiration to happiness which God has placed in the heart of every man; it takes up the hopes that inspire men's activities and purifies them so as to order them to the Kingdom of heaven; it keeps man from discouragement; it sustains him during times of abandonment; it opens up his heart in expectation of eternal beatitude. Buoyed up by hope, he is preserved from selfishness and led to the happiness that flows from charity. (*CCC*, 1818)

Just as the star the Magi follow will come to "rest over the place where the child was" (Matthew 2:9), so Jesus will reorder Joseph's world. I think it's safe to say that Joseph possesses a new understanding of heaven and earth as he obeys God's call. Like the Magi who pay homage to Jesus, Joseph will, for the rest of his life, place everything he has and all that he is at Jesus's feet.

There is no indication in Scripture that Joseph ever questioned how Jesus would fulfill the hopes of God's people. Rather, we can see from Joseph's actions his strong conviction about the destiny of the child who would be known as "the son of Joseph" (John 1:45; 6:42). No doubt the angel's words guided and shaped the way in which Joseph aided Jesus's growth to manhood. In every word and gesture toward Jesus, Joseph must have been looking toward the fulfillment of those words.

Joseph shows us that hope engages us in the plan of God. We don't stand by as idle spectators waiting to see God's plan unfold. Rather, hope draws us toward God in our desire to be saved from our sins. It stirs our hearts and minds to recognize the ways in which we can serve God within the concrete conditions of our lives. That's certainly what Joseph experienced.

HOPE FOR THE WORLD

While every child should be raised in an atmosphere of hope, the child Jesus is the source of the hope in which he is raised. Just as every child naturally arouses a sense of what might be—moving us beyond our limitations and experiences—the child Jesus points us toward a future that only he can bring about. While the smile of a child—even if but for a moment—casts aside uncertainty and fear and renews a belief in what's best about humanity, the smile of Mary's child touches the deepest longings of our hearts. This is the child who causes the angels to sing, "On earth peace among men with whom [God] is pleased" (Luke 2:14).

Only hardened and indifferent hearts can remain unmoved in the presence of a child. For such men and women, hope has died. All that's left is a passive resignation to the passage of time. Sadly, this is the condition of many in our world today. They have perhaps unwittingly replaced hope with a reliance on "evolutionary progress" or the naïve belief that humanity can bring about a better future by its own initiatives.

St. Joseph is a fitting antidote to the widespread atheism and agnostic humanism that plague our world. His life reveals for us that faith and hope are inseparable, that they are bound together by God's initiative to reach toward the human family in love. This was, for Joseph, no abstract idea. In the peacefulness of a sleep most assuredly having God as its source (as with Adam in Genesis 2:21), Joseph learned that God's movement toward humanity is highly personal. God does not act outside of our lives but rather within them.

Hope is the fruit of being touched by God's saving love in Christ. It is an ever-deepening anticipation of Christ's coming and how it will affect us. This establishes Joseph as a most fitting guardian of the Incarnation. He reminds us that the Incarnation is not over. It is not an event restrained by time but the opening of time to the grace of the child who will save us all from our sins.

Hope does not disguise or disfigure the present; it gives the present its proper perspective. As St. Paul tells the Christian community in Rome, "Hope does not disappoint us, because God's love has been poured into our hearts through the Holy Spirit who has been given to us" (Romans 5:5).

Joseph was particularly blessed in that he could never mistake the hiddenness of God for the absence of God. Whenever he looked upon the child Jesus, the words of the shepherds (Luke 2:15–20) and of Anna and Simeon (Luke 2:22–38) and the actions of the Magi (Matthew 2:10–12) no doubt filled his mind with anticipatory wonder. Joseph heard amazing things said of Jesus, who in turn pointed Joseph to the Father.

Yet in order to possess this new hope stirred by the presence of Mary's child, Joseph needed to freely yield his life to God's plan of redemption. Freedom is the key to the opening of Joseph's life to the new covenant. In the beautiful interplay between God's freedom and Joseph's freedom, all that is specifically human—responsibility, intelligence, desire, weakness, limitation, vulnerability, and confidence—is taken up by God for the purpose of history. Thus hope fixes Joseph's gaze on the future, on a destiny that is not simply the development of the created order according to human ingenuity and artifice but rather "the final realization of the unity of the human race" (*CCC*, 1045).[15]

Scripture indicates that Joseph did not witness the sacrifice of love that is the source of human salvation. The last incident in which Joseph participates is the finding of the twelve-year-old Jesus in the Temple. St. John tells us that Mary was at the foot of the cross, and Jesus entrusted her to "the disciple whom he loved," indicating that she was a widow (John 19:25–27).

I would suggest that witnessing the cross was unnecessary for Joseph. All of us born into the life of Christ after his passion, death, and resurrection are called, as was Joseph, to live by faith and not by sight. Joseph's life so wonderfully illustrates that, even though "We know *neither the moment of the consummation* of the earth and of man, nor the way in which the universe will be transformed," hope enables us to live in the world with an "expectancy of a new earth" that spurs us on toward "the better ordering of human society" (*CCC*, 1048–1049).[16] The hope that grounds our lives assures us that the world and each one of us, distorted by sin, are even now being transformed by the power of the Spirit.

Joseph encourages us to let hope sustain our lives and secure them in the God who loves us "to the end" (John 13:1). As we have access to Christ through his body the Church, hope should likewise be the foundation of our lives.

Joseph passed from this world knowing the only true God through, with, and in the boy he raised to manhood. The Church encourages us "to entrust ourselves to St. Joseph, the patron of a happy death" (*CCC*, 1014). Having lived in hope from the moment he welcomed Mary into his home, Joseph was welcomed into eternal life in "the definitive realization of God's plan" (*CCC*, 1043).

CHAPTER SIX

MAN OF CHARITY

Beloved, let us love one another; for love is of God, and he who loves is born of God and knows God. He who does not love does not know God; for God is love. In this the love of God was made manifest among us: that God sent his only-begotten Son into the world, so that we might live through him. In this is love, not that we loved God but that he loved us and sent his Son to be expiation for our sins. Beloved, if God so loved us, we also ought to love one another. (1 John 4:7–11)

ST. JOSEPH TRULY DEDICATED HIS life to "the love that never ends" (*CCC*, 25).[17] Even before his betrothal to Mary, he regarded all men and women through the prism of the universal fatherhood of God. Both the Law and the prophets required him to act with justice toward all, especially widows, aliens, and orphans.

You shall not wrong a stranger or oppress him, for you were strangers in the land of Egypt. You shall not afflict any widow or orphan. (Exodus 22:21)

At the end of every three years you shall bring forth all the tithe of your produce in the same year, and lay it up within your towns; and the Levite, because he has no portion or inheritance with you, and the sojourner, the fatherless, and the widow, who are within your towns, shall come and eat and be filled; that the LORD your God may bless you in all the work of your hands that you do. (Deuteronomy 14:28–29)

If you do not oppress the alien, the fatherless or the widow, or shed innocent blood in this place, and if you do not go after other gods to your own hurt, then I will let you dwell in this place, in the land that I gave of old to your fathers for ever. (Jeremiah 7:6–7)

By his obedience Joseph was suitably predisposed for the "Law of the Gospel," which "fulfills, refines, surpasses, and leads the Old Law to its perfection" (*CCC*, 1967).[18] Yet his transition from the old order to the new wasn't seamless. He had to live the new commandment of Jesus, to "love one another as [he] has loved [us]" (John 15:12), during the unsettling conflict caused by the news of Mary's condition. In the instant of that revelation, Joseph's natural love and concern for Mary was at enmity with the demands of the Law by which he ordered his life. How could he expose Mary to a shame to which he himself would not wish to be exposed (see Matthew 7:12)? And the penalty for what seemed to be her sin was death—by stoning.

Matthew's Gospel hints at how heavily this dilemma weighed upon Joseph's heart. For even after he "resolved to send her away quietly," he continued to "consider this" (Matthew 1:19, 20).

This internal conflict produces the opening through which God aims to elevate and orient Joseph's human love. The angel comes in a dream not only to explain how Mary came to be with child but to offer Joseph a part in God's saving plan. Through the power of the Spirit, who has overshadowed Mary, a new covenant is offered. God's law will be put into the minds and hearts of his people:

Behold, the days are coming, says the LORD, when I will make a new covenant with the house of Israel and the house of Judah, not like the covenant which I made with their fathers when I took them by the hand to bring them out of the land of Egypt, my covenant which they broke, and I showed myself their Master says the LORD. But this is the covenant which I will make with the house of Israel after those days, says the LORD.... I will put my law within them, and I will write it upon their hearts; and I will be their God, and they shall be my people. And no longer shall each man teach his neighbor and each his brother, saying, "Know the LORD," for they shall all know me, from the least of them to the greatest, says the LORD; for I will forgive their iniquity, and I will remember their sin no more. (Jeremiah 31:31–32, 33–34)

The angel shows Joseph the way through his internal conflict; it is a way that requires a new understanding of what it means to love God and love one's neighbor.

In fact, God here reveals himself as man's neighbor, for the child will "save his people from their sins" (Matthew 1:21). By welcoming Mary and her child, Joseph crosses the threshold from the old law and steps into the kingdom of the new.

LOVE IN ACTION

Joseph will continue to discover how the law of love is always occasioned by sacrifice and at times real suffering. He will experience the demand to look beyond himself and his needs and truly see the other. By keeping his mind and heart set on his responsibility toward Mary and Jesus, Joseph experiences and expresses the love that "bears all things, believes all things, hopes all things, endures all things" (1 Corinthians 13:7).

Joseph's first exposure to this truth of Christian charity is prompted by Jesus's birth. The utter humility by which the eternal God is born into the world already points toward the sacrifice by which Christ will die for love of us. The discomfiting conditions in Bethlehem might surely have caused others to demand that God look to their needs. Yet Mary and Joseph never take their attention off the child to be born, Jesus, "the Son of the Most High" (Luke 1:32).

They watch God enter the world in absolute material poverty. How concretely they must recognize that they can only return to the child the love that God has given them. "In this is love, not that we loved God but that he loved us and sent his Son to be the expiation for our sins" (1 John 4:10).

As Mary wraps Jesus in swaddling clothes and places him in the manger, both she and Joseph know that loving this child, who is "God become neighbor," is the single norm by which their lives will be judged. Jesus will be raised by parents whose every word and deed genuinely convey the fact that love is the fulfillment of the Law.

> Owe no one anything, except to love one another; for he who loves his neighbor has fulfilled the law. The commandments, "You shall not commit adultery, You shall not kill, You shall not steal, You shall not covet," and any other commandment, are summed up in this sentence, "You shall love your neighbor as yourself." Love does no wrong to a neighbor; therefore love is the fulfilling of the law. (Romans 13:8–10)

> For the whole law is fulfilled in one word, "You shall love your neighbor as yourself." (Galatians 5:14).

At Jesus's birth Mary and Joseph come to experience concretely the truth that love of God and love of one's neighbor are inseparable. As the apostle John will say, "He who does not love his brother whom he has seen, cannot love God whom he has not seen" (1 John 4:20). At his home in Nazareth, Jesus will be raised in "a school of human virtues and of Christian charity" (*CCC*, 1666), by a man and woman who look upon him and see the human face of God.

Far from causing Mary and Joseph to become isolated and introspective, this revelation of God as neighbor actually positions them to share the love they have received with others. Mary has already demonstrated this by going in haste to visit her cousin Elizabeth, who has also been touched by God in a hoped for but unexpected way (see Luke 1:39–45). It will likewise be the case at the wedding in Cana, when Mary is the first to recognize the plight of the bride and groom (see John 2:1–12).

It is also the case here in Bethlehem with the shepherds, whose angelic experience compels them to go "and see this thing that has happened, which the Lord has made known to us" (Luke 2:15). Mary and Joseph recognize these "who are poor in the world" as "heirs of the kingdom which he has promised to those who love him" (James 2:5). They welcome the shepherds just as they will welcome the Magi, who will come with their "treasures…gold and frankincense and myrrh" (Matthew 2:11).

When the days for purification have been completed, Mary and Joseph demonstrate this love again by allowing a complete stranger to hold in his arms the child Jesus, the "consolation of Israel" for which he has longed (Luke 2:30). They in turn hear Simeon's amazing words about Jesus:

> Behold, this child is set for the fall and rising of many in
>   Israel,
> and for a sign that is spoken against
> (and a sword will pierce through your own soul also),

that thoughts out of many hearts may be revealed.
(Luke 2:34–35)

Mary and Joseph will cherish these words, reflect on them, and let them nourish this new law of love. This is what prayer and the reading of Scripture is meant to do for us. "Daily prayer and the reading of the Word strengthen [the Christian family] in charity" (*CCC,* 2205).

Joseph and Mary's openness to the many strangers who come to see Jesus anticipates Christ's teaching about love as the basis of the moral act.

> "I was a stranger, and you welcomed me...." "When did we see you a stranger and welcome you?..." "Truly, I say to you, as you did it to one of the least of these my brethren, you did it to me." (Matthew 25:35, 38, 40)

Their welcome also foreshadows the inextricable bond between the reception of the Eucharist and our responsibility to give others the "look of love which they crave."[19] Already in the home at Nazareth, Joseph and Mary are living "Eucharistic" lives. They have received Jesus, the sacrament of God, and have come to recognize that their lives are now united with all those whom he has come to save. Their reception of Christ spills over into the concrete practices of their daily lives. This is the real proof of their membership in the family of Jesus: "Whoever does the will of my Father in heaven is my brother, and sister, and mother" (Mathew 12:50).

LEARNING LOVE

While the explicit nature of Joseph's embrace of the new law of love has not been preserved for us in Scripture, it certainly can be gleaned from the life of the child he helped raise. Jesus's words about love extend from love of one's own to love of one's enemies (see Matthew 5:44).

Joseph was well aware that sin had rendered us enemies of God, but through the words of the angel and the birth of Mary's son, he knew that God's love for the human family was far greater than humanity's rejection of God. Jesus grew up in the home of a man who knew and lived the words "I desire mercy and not sacrifice" (Hosea 6:6).

Mary's overshadowing by the Most High extended to Joseph: His heart was overshadowed by charity. Through Mary and Jesus's presence, the love of God poured into Joseph's heart in tangible ways. He established a home in which the new law of God's love set the pattern of daily life. There Jesus would grow "in wisdom and in stature, and in favor with God and man" (Luke 2:51). Joseph would grow in the same grace, in a wisdom that would surpass human understanding.

CHAPTER SEVEN

MAN OF COURAGE

You are the salt of the earth; but if salt has lost its taste, how shall its saltiness be restored? It is no longer good for anything except to be thrown out and trodden under foot by men.

You are the light of the world. A city set on a hill cannot be hidden. Nor do men light a lamp and put it under a bushel, but on a stand, and it gives light to all in the house. Let your light so shine before men, that they may see your good works and give glory to your Father who is in heaven. (Matthew 5:13–16)

THE WORDS THAT JESUS SPEAKS during the course of his public ministry are not abstract theories about human behavior and the right ordering of society. Jesus is not a philosopher; he is the Son of God made man. His teachings emanate from his being one with the Father and, through the Spirit by which he took flesh, from his own personal history as a man. Jesus "invited" his "disciples…to live in the sight of the Father…in order to become 'perfect as your heavenly Father is perfect'" (*CCC*, 1693).[20]

This is an important point, especially as it pertains to the Sermon on the Mount (see Matthew 5—7). The Beatitudes are the essential focus of this discourse. They are not suggestions about human behavior, nor are they merely ideals toward which each of us must strive, nor are they an eight-step spiritual program for achieving eternal life. The

Beatitudes are first and foremost descriptive and not proscriptive. They frame for us the dispositions that characterize the fullness of life Jesus inaugurates by his coming to us as man.

As interior dispositions that express the Holy Spirit at work in the life of a believer (see Romans 5:3–5), the Beatitudes are inherently bound to the ongoing discovery of self that takes place in the light of the Incarnate Word. Accepting and therefore understanding our situation before God never ends; our absolute dependence upon him only deepens as we proceed on the pathway of life.

As this deepening takes place in our hearts, blessedness exhibits itself ever more in our relationships with others. Our stance before the world becomes wholly determined by the two great commandments of love of God and love for one's neighbor.

A MATTER OF THE HEART

Like charity, courage is born from a heart awakened to the truth of God present in the person of his Son. Joseph literally awakes to this truth and immediately sets about centering his life on the Incarnate Word. Even before Jesus is born, a transformation has begun in Joseph through the power of the Spirit in both Mary and her child. By their presence in his life, Joseph comes to understand God and himself in new and wondrous ways. This new way of seeing profoundly impacts this already righteous man, setting him on course to become a living embodiment of the blessedness Jesus describes in his famous sermon.

Far from being incapacitated by the angel's description of Mary's child, Joseph boldly accepts the responsibility with which he's been entrusted. He finds courage in adopting the meekness that Jesus will later espouse: "Take my yoke upon you, and learn from me; for I am gentle and lowly in heart, and you will find rest for your souls" (Matthew 11:29).

Courage equated with meekness may initially appear to be a contradiction, but in describing himself as gentle and lowly in heart, Jesus offers a corrective about genuine human strength: It is not an exercise of power as the world considers it; rather it is the honest recognition of one's own limitations, weaknesses, and vulnerability and of God's ability to use them to manifest strength.

Meekness is a willed commitment to "sympathy, love of the brethren, a tender heart and a humble mind." It does not "return evil for evil or reviling for reviling" but rather blesses (1 Peter 3:8, 9). Meekness, the antithesis of aggression, protects against the Evil One,

> Because he clings to me in love, I will deliver him;
> I will protect him, because he knows my name.
> When he calls to me, I will answer him;
> I will be with him in trouble,
> I will rescue him and honor him.
> With long life I will satisfy him,
> and show him my salvation. (Psalm 91:14–16)

Meekness yields the strength that only God can give the human person, beyond all human strength: "I can do all things in him who strengthens me" (Philippians 4:13). "In the Christian life," the *Catechism* tells us, "the Holy Spirit himself accomplishes his work by mobilizing the whole being" (*CCC*, 1769).

Meekness is the virtue for which Moses was known and celebrated. "Now the man Moses was very meek, more than all men that were on the face of the earth" (Numbers 12:3). And how the Lord worked through him!

> From his descendants the Lord brought forth a man of mercy,
> who found favor in the sight of all flesh

and was beloved by God and man,

Moses, whose memory is blessed.

He made him equal in glory to the holy ones,

and made him great in the fears of his enemies.

By his words he caused signs to cease;

the Lord glorified him in the presence of kings.

He gave him commands for his people,

and showed him part of his glory.

He sanctified him through faithfulness and meekness;

he chose him out of all mankind.

He made him hear his voice,

and led him into the thick darkness,

and gave him the commandments face to face,

the law of life and knowledge,

to teach Jacob the covenant,

and Israel his judgments. (Sirach 45:1–5)

Abide in Christ

The strength that flows from faith and is expressed by one's obedience to the Father is resolutely opposed to any behavior that would seek to control or manipulate others. The meek will come to inherit the land not by any external force or through self-centered motives but by the internal resolve to remain yoked with Christ. In being one with Christ, the world and all that's in it already belong to us, but not in the sense of a possession.

The meek have no desire to possess anyone or anything; God has so overcome them that the life they live is no longer their own (see Galatians 2:20). He has "increased" their "strength of soul" (Psalm 138:3). They can live for God because of the courage that comes from adoption into his life. They have begun "to comprehend with all the saints what is the breadth and length and height and depth, and to know the love of Christ which surpasses knowledge," to "be filled with all the fulness of God" (Ephesians 3:18–19).

St. Joseph is called Jesus's adoptive father, but when he took Mary and her child into his home, it's Joseph who was adopted into the life of God's family. By saying yes to the Father's plan, he accepted the "burden" of being yoked to Jesus (see Matthew 11:28–30). In that moment he opened himself to the inestimable reach of God's right hand and was imbued with the courage to remain steadfast.

Joseph could see clearly the futility of trying to achieve some sense of mastery over things that ultimately do not matter. He understood that the constant expense of energy and worry in fighting to gain or keep hold of others or the world is painfully wearisome and futile. "Which of you by being anxious can add one cubit to his span of life?" (Matthew 6:27).

It takes courage to hand over these ways of living, exhaustive as they are, in exchange for "the rest" God offers us in Christ.

> Therefore, while the promise of entering his rest remains, let us fear lest any of you be judged to have failed to reach it. For good news came to us just as to [the Israelites under Moses]; but the message which they heard did not benefit them, because it did not meet with faith in the hearers....
>
> Let us therefore strive to enter that rest, that no one fall by the same sort of disobedience. (Hebrews 4:1–2, 11)

While Joseph most assuredly had not built his life upon the ever shifting and disorienting ways of the world, the light of the Incarnate Word more clearly distinguished for him the futility of such ways.

Joseph was free of the risk of passive cynicism with respect to reality. The moment he tethered his life to Jesus through welcoming Mary into his home, he was empowered by God's Spirit to "bear all things, believe all things, hope all things, endure all things" (1 Corinthians 13:7).

Joseph knew that the Father was the source of the courage required to embrace his role in the divine plan of redemption. He believed that God had entrusted to Jesus everything necessary for this new way of life (see Matthew 11:27). As the child would grow, Joseph would increasingly discover that Jesus gladly offers all that he has received from the Father.

Joseph would be quick to tell us that anyone who is willing to stand with Jesus has the assurance that the Father will supply the good things needed to stay strong.

> Ask, and it will be given you; seek, and you will find; knock, and it will be opened to you. For every one who asks receives, and he who seeks finds, and to him who knocks it will be opened. Or what man of you, if his son asks him for bread, will give him a stone? Or if he asks for a fish, will give him a serpent? If you then, who are evil, know how to give good gifts to your children, how much more will your Father who is in heaven give good things to those who ask him! (Matthew 7:7–11)

Truly those who abide in Christ will want for nothing.

NIGHT FLIGHT

In our consideration of Joseph's courage in caring for Mary and Jesus, the flight to Egypt comes to mind. The decision to flee was not the decision of a desperate or timid man, afraid to confront the Roman armies. Joseph was a man of confidence, unafraid of "those who kill the body but cannot kill the soul" (Matthew 10:28). Remaining in Bethlehem and trying to elude Herod and his forces would have been foolhardy. And that was not the Lord's direction.

Joseph never questioned the angel who told him to take the child and his mother to Egypt (see Matthew 2:13); he was courageous enough to go without any specifics. Was there an angel to guide him? Did he have a map?

Joseph displayed courage and self-possession in marching into the unknown. He willingly took his place with Mary and Jesus, not retreating from the world and his responsibilities but engaging the world with them. Like a lamp set on a stand (see Matthew 5:15), Joseph's life radiates the confident assurance that St. Paul encourages Timothy to embrace:

> For this reason, I remind you to rekindle the gift of God that is within you through the laying on of my hands; for God did not give us a spirit of timidity but a spirit of power and love and self-control.
>
> Do not be ashamed then of testifying to our Lord, nor of me his prisoner, but take your share of suffering for the gospel in the power of God. (2 Timothy 1:6–8)

Joseph becomes a living witness of Mary's Magnificat. He accepts the strength of God's arm and is lifted up with the lowly. He is filled and sustained by the good things of God, and this faithful servant receives the help of God (see Luke 1:46–55). With the courage that comes from trusting God, Joseph comes to possess the lowliness of heart that is the hallmark of Jesus's own heart.

There were no selfish ends in Joseph's abandonment to the Father's plan; his goal was to see God's love revealed just as the angel said:

through the forgiveness of sins (see Matthew 1:21). While Joseph surely had his own ideas about the faithful execution of his duties toward Mary and Jesus, he knew that God was even more aware of their needs and more capable of providing for them.

Lowliness of heart emboldened Joseph to live without concern for the future or worries from the past. This fostered in Joseph the peaceful security that is the gift of Christ to his faithful disciples: "Peace I leave with you; my peace I give to you; not as the world gives do I give to you. Let not your hearts be troubled, neither let them be afraid" (John 14:27).

Joseph lived this peace even in the most trying circumstances. The courage with which he willingly took on the yoke of Christ brought stability in times of horrific and unforeseen circumstances. It also sustained his openness to God. It is a testimony to the internal self-awareness resulting from the Spirit's residence in his soul.

Lowliness of heart is a moral absolute for Christian discipleship. Learning from Jesus demands the subordination of our inclinations and desires to the will of the Father. It safeguards our perseverance in walking with the Lord toward the Father.

Joseph never wavered. Let us follow his example in walking steadily in the redemptive love that flowed in the home at Nazareth.

CHAPTER EIGHT

MAN OF POVERTY

Jesus enjoins his disciples to prefer him to everything and everyone, and bids them "renounce all that [they have]" for his sake and that of the Gospel. Shortly before his passion he gave them the example of the poor widow of Jerusalem who, out of her poverty, gave all that she had to live on. The precept of detachment from riches is obligatory for entrance into the Kingdom of heaven. (*CCC*, 2544)[21]

W HEN JESUS "EMPTIED HIMSELF, TAKING the form of a servant" (Philippians 2:7), he was born into a simple home. Although Joseph was in no way destitute, the humble conditions of Jesus's birth indicate that he was not a man of means. The offering Joseph brought at the time of Mary's purification, "a pair of turtledoves, or two young pigeons," was prescribed for those who could "not afford a lamb" (Luke 2:24; Leviticus 12:8).

For those living in the developed nations of the Western world, poverty is largely the lot of isolated and unfortunate individuals who, whether by choice or bad luck, lack the basic necessities of life. On a global level, we see more radical conditions of poverty, which can come to a kind of helplessness in the face of life's demands. Only in sacred Scripture do we see poverty as a distress that opens a person to God in humble, loving abandonment.

In the Old Testament poverty was, for a time, thought to be a divine chastisement, a retributive punishment for disobeying the precepts of God. Wealth and status were the reward of remaining faithful to God and a sign of his favor. Psalm 112, for example, says of the righteous, "Wealth and riches are in his house" (Psalm 112:3).

After the humiliating experience of the Babylonian Captivity, the Israelites' way of seeing poverty was transformed. By the time of Christ's birth, poverty was also seen as a religious condition synonymous with humility and piety. John the Baptist, for example, appears to have embraced poverty willingly: He wore "a garment of camel's hair" and ate "locusts and wild honey." And "Jerusalem and all Judea and all the region about the Jordan" went out to hear him preach and to be baptized (Matthew 3:4, 5–6).

GOD LOVES THE POOR

Poverty plays an essential role in Christian life. Christ himself took on this human distress. He loves the poor because they embody man's need for deliverance and because their distress predisposes them to his message. Once we accept the fact that we can never make our lives secure, once we admit our inadequacy, we can begin to live the way Jesus asked all his followers to live:

> Do not be anxious about your life, what you shall eat or what you shall drink, nor about your body, what you shall put on. Is not life more than food, and the body more than clothing? Look at the birds of the air: they neither sow nor reap nor gather into barns, and yet your heavenly Father feeds them. Are you not of more value than they? And which of you by being anxious can add one cubit to his span of life? And why are you anxious about clothing? Consider the lilies of the field,

how they grow; they neither toil nor spin; yet I tell you, even Solomon in all his glory was not clothed like one of these. But if God so clothes the grass of the field, which today is alive and tomorrow is thrown into the oven, will he not much more clothe you...? Therefore do not be anxious. (Matthew 6:25–31).

Human distress will never be completely abolished. Jesus said, "The poor you always have with you" (John 12:8); accepting that fact allows us to live in humble expectation of Christ's coming. It also frees us to dismiss the cares of this world with true spiritual detachment.

Do not lay up for yourselves treasures on earth, where moth and rust consume and where thieves break in and steal, but lay up for yourselves treasures in heaven where neither moth nor rust consumes and where thieves do not break in and steal. For where your treasure is, there will your heart be also. (Matthew 6:19–21).

Every Christian should be undemanding and frugal in the management of earthly goods. Just as there is no ultimate security in human life, regardless of humanity's technical achievements, so, too, the Church will always remain "poor" in a theological sense. We are all called to accept in faith and with confidence the abandonment in which Christ has preceded us by his death.

All Christ's faithful are to "direct their affections rightly, lest they be hindered in their pursuit of perfect charity by the use of worldly things and by an adherence to riches which is contrary to the spirit of evangelical poverty." (*CCC*, 2545)[22]

Those in consecrated life undertake the special form of poverty that the Church describes as an evangelical counsel. For centuries men and women have taken vows of poverty as a condition of their individual or community life. This makes their lives an incarnate sign of God's kingdom and disposes them to serve the well-being of their neighbor. They participate even now in the death to self that is the way to everlasting life.

Perhaps the clearest depiction of the Christian response to poverty is found in the twenty-fifth chapter of St. Matthew's Gospel. After leaving the Temple area, Jesus's disciples approach him privately to ask how they will know that the end has come. On the Mount of Olives, where he delivered his sermon on the Beatitudes, Jesus describes the judgment of the nations in similar fashion.

The ones "blessed by [his] Father" (verse 34) live their love for God by caring for those lacking in basic human needs. Feeding and clothing, comforting and visiting, are the means by which the blessed address the reality of human poverty. Jesus presents the reward of God's kingdom as being rooted not in moral or ethical perfection, religious devotion, or pious sentiment but in one's responsiveness to the destitution of others.

As Jesus compellingly points out, the righteous are completely unaware of what awaits them (verse 37). Their lives, "exalted" and "filled…with good things" (Luke 1:52, 53), outwardly express the love they have received from God. Theirs is a natural attentiveness to the needs of others, coming from their own hunger, thirst, and outright need for God's providential comfort and care. Their poverty of spirit is the empty pool that can be filled with the life of God. Matthew 25 reveals how such souls have all along been living in the kingdom, though perhaps unknowingly.

All four Gospels noticeably relate poverty as a central theme of Jesus's public ministry, from its beginning to its conclusion. Having little or no money, possessions, or means of support serves as a tangible sign of the human condition as a result of sin. Being alienated from God has left each one of us impoverished, for we lack that which is essential to human flourishing: divine life.

Sin has also robbed us of our ability to steward creation on its journey to its state of perfection and blinded us to the needs of others. Now it is only through our incorporation into the life of Christ and the conversion of our hearts that the world will be transformed. Communion with Christ empowers us to order and manage every facet of our lives according to the love that constitutes his own. The eternally begotten Son of God comes into the world to enrich the human family with the gift of God's love and life.

A HUMBLE HOME

Known more for his profession than his possessions (see Matthew 13:55), Joseph was entrusted with the vital task of structuring Jesus's family life. This was a firsthand experience of what it means to renounce all things for the sake of the Gospel. Jesus sees in Joseph who gives to God "all the living [he] had" (see Luke 21:4). Jesus's first and greatest sermon describes the characteristics of the man and woman who fed, clothed, comforted, housed, and educated him, and helped him grow to manhood.

Establishing a home for his wife and her child meant more to Joseph than merely doing what the angel had commanded. He showed himself a "complete" man, "equipped for every good work" (2 Timothy 3:17). We saw when Joseph learned of Mary's condition that his respect for her, his discretion, and his heartfelt sensitivity to her "impoverished" state ruled the day. Our first introduction to him in Matthew's Gospel proves that he possessed the poverty of spirit later to be praised by Mary's son (Matthew 5:3).

The home God wanted for Jesus and his mother could only be provided by a true "son of David" (Matthew 1:20). Joseph was naturally unaware of his part in God's plan of salvation; he was dealing with great things he did not understand, "things too wonderful" to know (Job 42:3). Thus the angel of God was sent to open Joseph's ears to the truth of how the child came to be conceived in Mary.

> For God speaks in one way,
>   and in two, though man does not perceive it.
> In a dream, in a vision of the night,
>   when deep sleep falls upon men,
>   while they slumber on their beds,
>   then he opens the ears of men. (Job 33:14–16)

The angel of the Lord reassured Joseph that his home was the right place for the one who would "save his people from their sins" (Matthew 1:21). Rather than question how any of this could be, on waking Joseph "did as the angel of the Lord commanded him; he took his wife" into his home (Matthew 1:24).

The Lord saw fit to have Mary and her unborn child welcomed into a home in which affections were rightly ordered. The quiet laborer to whom Mary was betrothed was no passive bystander to the events foretold by the angel Gabriel. This humble carpenter provided for and protected Mary and the child in that immaculate grace that had already spilled into his life.

The simple home in Nazareth was a place of reverence for the Law, simplicity of life, and respect for human labor. The months of Mary's pregnancy were also a sort of gestation period for St. Joseph. The grace flowing from Mary and her child daily strengthened and expanded the natural virtues that made Joseph the right man to stand in place of the Father and raise his Son. Joseph earnestly attended to Mary's needs each day, and together they awaited the birth of Jesus.

Joseph and Mary were fortunate to have such privileged time together. Surely their sense of amazement at the scope of what was happening in their lives must have taken root in each of their hearts. God had not left them alone. Already there was a small community around the child whose life would fulfill "what was spoken by the prophets" (Matthew 2:23).

We can imagine that Joseph had time for private reflection about these matters while working as a carpenter. And what mutual prayer and encouragement he and Mary must have enjoyed as together they awaited the unfolding of God's plan.

Joseph's life was forever changed by his wiliness to do what the angel commanded. Since in Christ all are "renewed in the spirit" of the mind (Ephesians 4:23), Joseph must have come to entirely new ways of relating to God, himself, others, and all creation. As Joseph helped Jesus grow to manhood in preparation for his public ministry, he would grow in grace and wisdom along with the Son (see Luke 2:52).

Joseph knows firsthand how essential it is that we take Mary into our homes. He even now wants to help each believer order, manage, and build a suitable "home" for Mary and her son. For each believer that home is the heart, "our hidden center...the place of truth...the place of encounter...the place of covenant" (*CCC*, 2563). It is where we make our decision for God.

TRULY BLESSED

The life Joseph shared with Mary and Jesus in the home at Nazareth is the life God wants for all Christians. It is the school of the Beatitudes, where "the poor in spirit" are truly "blessed...for theirs is the kingdom of heaven" (Matthew 5:3). The meek likewise "inherit the land" that is the kingdom. It is a place of strength free of the desire to control, manipulate, or dominate others.

We live in a world beset with suspicion, duplicity, and antagonism. Ours is an age that champions the expression "Every man for himself." However, this is in fact the battle cry of those enslaved by concupiscence. The perversity in our culture is confirmed by a nearly universal willingness to celebrate and reward vengeance and treachery (just watch *Survivor* or follow politics). Even people of faith have come to accept the notion that no good deed goes unpunished.

But the good deeds of St. Joseph were never punished! This man of humility and simplicity "let the peace of Christ rule in [his] heart" (Colossians 3:15). And whatever Joseph did, "in word or deed," he did "in the name of the Lord Jesus, giving thanks to God the Father through him" (Colossians 3:17). St. Joseph is therefore a great champion for us as we seek to live in the world with our hearts set on higher things—not lofty ideas or noble sentiments but the child he took into his home and the kingdom that child brings.

Joseph is a constant example of poverty of spirit, expressed in his disposition and his manner of life. He was attentive to God and responsive to his commands. I think the fact that no words of Joseph have been recorded in the Scriptures is evidence of his graciousness and self-possession.

Jesus bears witness to this when, in the presence of the woman caught in adultery, his first response is to say nothing. Rather he bends down and silently traces lines in the sand (John 8:6). We can assume that, at his home in Nazareth, everyone was "quick to hear, slow to speak, slow to anger" (James 1:19).

In all things pertaining to his responsibility to care for Mary and Jesus, Joseph was not a "hearer that forgets but a doer that acts" (James 1:25). Jesus and his mother were his greatest treasure. His love and devotion provided a sense of stability and peace. Joseph's poverty of spirit enriched Mary and Jesus's life. Its light shone both in Egypt and at the home in Nazareth.

Joseph's home was built on the solid foundation of confidence in God. This environment preserved to some human measure the status that Jesus relinquished in being incarnate of the Blessed Virgin Mary. He "emptied himself, taking the form of a servant, being born in the likeness of men" (Philippians 2:7), yet his home was "good and pleasant," a place of "unity" (Psalm 133:1).

Christ became poor to make us rich (see 1 Corinthians 16:1; 2 Corinthians 8:9). The Father prepared more than just a body for him; he prepared a family. At the head of this family was a man who understood life's true worth and ultimate value. "Without pay" Joseph received from God the ultimate gift; "without pay" Joseph shared this gift with the world (Matthew 10:8).

The Father entrusted to Joseph the health and well-being of his Son. Thus the Father ensured that Jesus would be raised in a home that honored and expressed the eternal verities of his Godhead. From this stage would the Savior begin his work of healing a broken, wounded, suffering, and impoverished people.

CHAPTER NINE

MAN OF PURITY

Do not love the world or the things in the world. If anyone loves the world, love for the Father is not in him. For all that is in the world, the lust of the flesh and the lust of the eyes and the pride of life, is not of the Father but is of the world. And the world passes away, and the lust of it, but he who does the will of God abides for ever. (1 John 2:15–17)

W HEN A MAN AND WOMAN give themselves to one another in the sacrament of holy matrimony, the words of consent are meant to frame the whole of their life together. Their social standings, physical conditions, and personal shortcomings should never control or influence the love that effects their one-flesh unity. Through the grace of the sacrament, they are to become a living and tangible sign of the life of God, which is love. Therefore the promises they make to one another will be upheld only to the extent that they entrust their lives to God, each living for the other and never for self alone.

Be subject to one another out of reverence for Christ. Wives, be subject to your husbands, as to the Lord. For the husband is the head of the wife as Christ is the head of the Church, his body, and is himself its Savior.... Husbands, love your wives, as Christ loved the Church and gave himself up for her, that he might sanctify her, having cleansed her by the washing of water with the word, that he might present the Church to himself in splendor, without spot or wrinkle or any such thing, that she might be holy and without blemish. Even so husbands should love their wives as their own bodies. (Ephesians 5:21–23, 25–28)

PARADISE LOST

Christian marriage is not an antiquated religious institution that can be reconfigured by the whimsy of society. The meaning of marriage transcends all social customs and societal needs; it is only properly understood within the context of faith. When marriage is no longer grounded in the One who created man and woman after his own image and likeness, human sexuality is subject to destructive alterations due to a disordered vision of reality. Rather than seeing the world and the things of this world against the horizon of the divine, the focus shifts toward a narrow preoccupation with the self. Physical urges and emotional drives are exalted as needs that must be satisfied and never denied. This leads to what St. John describes as "the lust of the flesh and the lust of the eyes and the pride of life."

The enduring effects of original sin have had a destructive influence on human creation and on man's ability to incarnate God's love. In the aftermath of the so-called "sexual revolution"—involving naïve attempts to be freed from the constraints of allegedly outdated sexual mores—sex is no longer regarded as a beautiful and privileged way of "speaking" love to the other. Many people today think of sex as merely another activity of the body, like eating, sleeping, and eliminating.

What's been lost is the inherent meaning of the male and female bodies. It is left to the individual to determine the meaningfulness of his or her sexual acts, which society tries to tell us are in themselves entirely neutral. The sense of mystery and transcendence is obfuscated by a radical preoccupation with the fulfillment of desires. The modern man sees only himself; his constant state of impurity prevents him from seeing God.

Sadly, many Christian communities have embraced theories about sexual expression and gender that alienate them from the God who created them male and female. The theology that has been written into the mystery of the human body has been whitewashed by the same dubiousness with which the serpent pushed Eve to question whether or not God really told her to "not eat of any tree of the garden" (Genesis 3:1). The God of this "modern Christianity" would never tell a person no, especially when it comes to whom we love and how we express our love.

The collapse of married life and love is an unmistakable sign of this age's need for a clean heart and renewed spirit. The true end of man is the God who asked a simple carpenter to raise the Savior of mankind within the context of chaste marital love. Joseph not only opened his home to Mary and Jesus; he offered them his heart. Through the union of their lives, orchestrated by God, Joseph's heart was cleansed in the outpouring of the grace of the Holy Spirit.

Joseph held before his very eyes the one who is himself the ultimate enticement of the human heart. His yes to the Father's plan echoed in the life he shared with Mary and Jesus, just as the "I do" of marital consent resounds in the daily life of the Christian couple. Purified by Mary's love and then the love of her son, Joseph cared for them both with an upright and undivided heart.

Joseph's chaste love of Mary freed him from the bonds of concupiscence. Sensual lust had no place in the home at Nazareth. The sole pride of Joseph's life was the privilege of caring for Jesus and his mother. An ongoing purification of vision assured Joseph's ability to recognize and fulfill the will of God in everything.

Purity, like faith, is a virtue that describes how a person sees reality. For those who are pure of heart, all self-interest is pushed aside, in the same way that a man leaves his mother and father and becomes one with his wife (see Matthew 19:4–6). The pure of heart are captivated by the beauty of the created order. They appropriately exercise the dominion over it that God originally entrusted to the human family. Purity affirms the goodness God acknowledged in everything he created. It paves the way for the renewal of "the life and culture of fallen man" (*CCC*, 2527).[23]

Jesus tells us that the pure of heart are blessed because "they shall see God" (Matthew 5:8). Who better appreciates his words than Mary and Joseph? They were the first to behold the human face of God. Now they see all things accordingly. Joseph and Mary accept others as their neighbors, extending the love that brought them together as man and wife. The union of their lives in the love conceived in Mary's womb enhances their perception of the human body "as a temple of the Holy Spirit, a manifestation of divine beauty" (*CCC*, 2519).

PURE PATRONAGE

Because of their purity of heart, Mary and Joseph can "read" the theology of the human body. They fully appreciate the dignity of human sexuality as first and foremost a language, not an activity. They understand the body's capacity to express love within its appropriate context. Joseph is the rightful guardian of Jesus and Mary, and so he is the guardian of all who desire to live pure lives.

The example of Joseph's life highlights what is sorely needed today: an unyielding refusal "to unveil what should remain hidden" (*CCC*, 2521). Ours is a culture that discourages modesty and propriety in the mistaken assumption that everyone has the right to know everything about everyone else. Lines of decorum and decency have been blurred.

In far too many dimensions of human life, there exists an inordinate desire to burden others with what should remain intimate and personal.

Today private lives are thrust into the domain of what's public, and those who resist such impositions as religiously unacceptable or personally discomforting are branded intolerant and cruel. We are expected to rejoice in and acknowledge others' loves and expressions of love. All too often this involves the sacrifice of the dignity of the human person.

Although we have limited details about St. Joseph's life, we can be sure of his patronage in the purification that our social climate desperately needs. Perhaps more than any other essential Christian figure, he champions the purity of heart that can free the modern world from the embrace of eroticism for the celebration of true beauty. As he embraced his life with Mary and Jesus, so can we today come to appreciate the richness, complexity, and mystery of reality.

The reigning concern of Joseph and all those who are pure of heart is to fortify, restore, and complete all things in Christ. This is attendant upon all Christian men and women. In terms of social media, we must insist upon and strive for respect and restraint. We must nudge the arts to reject all forms of voyeurism and search for true magnificence.

Just as Joseph's life was completed by the child he raised to adulthood, so will the life of any person who seeks Jesus be free from the enslavement to sin. Joseph is the embodiment of reverence and self-control because he allowed God to cleanse and renew his heart.

St. Joseph is a man of purity precisely because he availed himself of the moral law that the child presents. With Mary and Jesus beside him, Joseph could withstand the erroneous conception of human freedom as the fulfillment of any desire of the human will.

Joseph is a pure-hearted man because he accepted the will of God. The movement of the Spirit in his life yielded both decency and discretion. He was content to serve God's plan by serving Mary and Jesus. Through them and in them, Joseph daily beheld the face of God, and from that he never looked away.

CHAPTER TEN

MAN OF PRAYER

Pray then like this:
Our Father who art in heaven,
Hallowed be thy name.
Thy kingdom come.
Thy will be done,
    On earth as it is in heaven.
Give us this day our daily bread;
And forgive us our trespasses,
    As we forgive those who trespass against us;
And lead us not into temptation,
    But deliver us from evil.
For if you forgive men their trespasses, your heavenly Father also will forgive you; but if you do not forgive men their trespasses, neither will your Father forgive your trespasses. (Matthew 6:9–15)

FROM THE START OF HIS public ministry, Jesus frequently goes off by himself to a quiet place and prays. What takes place during these solitary moments does not go unnoticed by the apostles. They ask him to teach them how to pray, just as John the Baptist taught his disciples (see Luke 11:1).

The apostles instinctively realize that something remarkable is taking place in Jesus's prayer, and they want to experience it for themselves. "In seeing the Master at prayer the disciple of Christ also wants to pray. By *contemplating* and hearing the Son, the master of prayer, the children learn to pray to the Father" (*CCC*, 2601).

Genuine prayer is attractive. Each one of us has been created for the same type of intensive experience that the apostles witnessed and would soon come to live. When Jesus simply and directly responds to their request, he entrusts them and thus the Church with "the fundamental Christian prayer" (*CCC*, 2759), a set of seven direct petitions.

Jesus has not given us "a formula to repeat mechanically" (*CCC*, 2766). "The Lord's Prayer 'is truly the summary of the whole gospel'" (*CCC*, 2761).[24] Its petitions are meant to guide the interior conversation with the Father that the Spirit makes possible. This is what we are to say to God when we retreat into the interiority of our hearts to converse with him.

Jesus's response to the apostles' request also recalls for us the fact that prayer is a gift from God. "O Lord, open my lips," David prayed, "and my mouth shall show forth your praise" (Psalm 51:15). "Even after losing through his sin his likeness to God, man remains an image of his Creator, and retains the desire for the one who calls him into existence" (*CCC*, 2566).

We can forget or reject God, we can establish idols for ourselves, we can come up with our own ideas about the meaning of human existence, but God remains ever present, tirelessly calling each individual person to an encounter with his love.

God's refusal to leave us cut off from his life is the basis of prayer. Our prayer is always a human response to God's call. "Whether we realize it or not, prayer is the encounter of God's thirst with ours. God thirsts that we may thirst for him" (*CCC*, 2560).[25]

The apostles learned through Jesus's words and parables that prayer is more than merely a religious activity; it is a way of life. They witnessed Jesus's habit of being in the presence of God and in steady communion with him. Their own hearts were profoundly touched by Jesus's every word and gesture. They learned through Jesus's example that prayer flows from the heart, the hidden center of man and the dwelling place of truth. By keeping their hearts rooted in God they would live in and experience the communion that made Jesus's life so attractive. When Jesus taught them how to pray, he was teaching them how to live.

FAMILY PRAYER

Before Jesus undertook his public ministry, he "learned to pray according to his human heart." God entrusted this task to his parents. Mary taught Jesus "the formulas of prayer," and we can assume that Joseph took responsibility to teach him "to pray in the words and rhythms of the prayer of his people, in the synagogue at Nazareth and the Temple at Jerusalem" (*CCC*, 2599). This was an extremely important fatherly duty, part of handing down the Law:

> And these words which I command you this day shall be upon your heart; and you shall teach them diligently to your children, and shall talk of them when you sit in your house, and when you walk by the way, and when you lie down, and when you rise. (Deuteronomy 6:6–7)

Joseph was one of the first to see the uniqueness of Jesus's prayer expressed. It certainly couldn't have been easy to tell Jesus to return to Nazareth when Jesus felt that he "must be in [his] Father's house" (Luke 2:49). This was Joseph's first experience of the "filial prayer" coursing through the human heart of the twelve-year-old boy.

Here the newness of prayer in the fullness of time begins to be revealed: his *filial prayer*, which the Father awaits from his children, is finally going to be lived out by the only Son in his humanity, with and for men. (*CCC,* 2599)

The family life in Nazareth would be the backdrop of the prayer later manifested in Jesus's public ministry. This indicates that Joseph was himself a man of deep prayer. Like his forefather Abraham, Joseph submitted his life to the word of God. His heart was attentive to the Lord, an essential element of prayer.

Abraham was so attentive to God that he was willing to sacrifice Isaac, the son whom God had given him as the inheritor of the promise, believing that "God was able to raise men even from the dead" (Hebrews 11:19). Joseph was attentive to God in welcoming Mary into his home. God led both men to places unknown and unexpected. Each went obediently because it was God asking them to go.

The plan of God expressed by the angel and incarnate in Mary's son no doubt influences Joseph's experience of prayer as a member of God's people. He no doubt prayed the psalms. By the time Jesus was conceived, these had already been collected into the five books called the "Praises." "The psalms both nourished and expressed the prayer of the People of God gathered during the great feasts at Jerusalem and each Sabbath in the synagogues" (*CCC,* 2586).

Having arisen from the communities of the Holy Land and those of the Diaspora, the psalms embrace all of creation while being always both personal and communal. They recall the saving events of God in the past while at the same time looking ahead to the future, including the end of time. The psalms celebrate the promises God has kept, even as they anticipate their definitive fulfillment in the person of the Messiah.

The psalms and their attendant messages would have formed a substantial part of Joseph's prayer life prior to and during his betrothal to Mary. After God's intervention in Nazareth, these prayers took on new meaning for Joseph, as they were directed toward the child conceived through the power of the Holy Spirit. The "simplicity and spontaneity of prayer; the desire for God himself through and with all that is good in his creation; the distraught situation of the believer who, in his preferential love for the Lord, is exposed to a host of enemies and temptations, but who waits upon what the faithful God will do, in the certitude of his love and in submission to his will" (*CCC*, 2589) now will be interpreted according to the events that take place in the life of Jesus. Joseph and Mary become the first members of the new covenant to pray the psalms within the light of Christ. Together they prepare the way for all men and women to speak to the Father with and in the Son, by the power of the Holy Spirit.

Subtly and without force, Joseph's prayer becomes ever more centered on Jesus. While remaining a faithful member of God's people and adhering to all the requirements of the Law, Joseph is nonetheless able to see and comprehend those requirements from an entirely new perspective. In this he not only apprehends the God of his ancestors but also garners greater insights into the history of his people.

Everything Joseph knew is amended by the presence of Jesus. Like the burning bush from which God called out to Moses in the desert (see Exodus 3:4), God will persistently call out to Joseph in Jesus, asking him to be an associate in the work of salvation. Just as the burning bush was not consumed by the fire of the divine presence, so is God's presence not consumed by the flesh of Mary's son. Just as Moses was drawn to the mystery of the burning bush, Joseph will be drawn to the mystery of God that is Jesus and spend his life in service to that mystery. Joseph is a model of Christian prayer because, like Moses, Joseph was able to speak with God as one friend speaks to another (Exodus 33:11).

Whatever questions Joseph may have had about the scope of God's plan for Jesus and of Joseph's own role in that plan, we can assume that he freely addressed them to the Father. And Jesus's presence in Joseph's life allowed an unprecedented conversation to take place between Joseph and the God of Abraham, Isaac, and Jacob. This establishes Joseph as more than just the patriarchs' equal. His life is fixed in the genealogy Matthew recounts, not as a footnote but as its climax. Matthew presents Joseph within the context of the past while showing him to be a central figure in the present and in Jesus's return in glory. Joseph's life of prayer beautifully incorporates that of God's people while at the same time exposing the light of God's redemptive love present in the child.

PRAYING WITH MARY

The influence of Jesus upon Joseph's experience of and thoughts about prayer cannot be overstated. Nor can the influence of Jesus's mother. We can say that Joseph's prayer becomes both Christ-centered and Marian. The woman to whom he is betrothed "shows the way" of prayer. Through her unique cooperation with the working of the Holy Spirit, she is able to help Joseph center on the person of her son.

Because of Mary, Joseph's relationship with God exists on an exceptionally new level. Mary's presence helps secure for Joseph the same type of relationship with God that was previously thought to be reserved to Abraham, Isaac, Jacob, Moses, the great prophets, and King David. It is owing to Mary and to obedience to God's plan that Joseph rightly takes his place in the company of these icons of Israel's past. Joseph's life of prayer will be sustained by Mary and united with her in hope.

Mary is the perfect *Orans* (pray-er), a figure of the Church. When we pray to her, we are adhering with her to the plan of the Father, who sends his Son to save all men. Like the beloved disciple, we welcome Jesus' mother into our homes, for she has become the mother of all the living. We can pray with and to her. The prayer of the Church is sustained by the prayer of Mary and united with it in hope. (*CCC*, 2679).[26]

Joseph's prayer life also points to the intimacy he shares with God. The dreams recorded in Scripture attest to this. Joseph seems to have no trouble accepting the fact that the thoughts and directions he receives in his sleep have God as their source. Only a man who is attuned to the Lord of the living would be able to distinguish that which comes from God and that which is from man.

The Old Testament Joseph was also noted for his sensitivity to the movements and desires of God expressed through dreams. God spoke to this patriarch in dreams, and he was able to interpret other people's dreams. In the quiet and calm of sleep, his life was open to God's regenerative and sustaining love. How interesting that the earthly father of the Messiah would share this gift with the man who shared his name and saved his people from famine.

CONTEMPLATIVE PRAYER

The decisiveness with which Joseph acts upon his dreams (see Matthew 1:24; 2:14, 21) reveals a man who already walks with God. The intimacy between Joseph and the Father of his people is transformed by the presence of Jesus into what the Christian tradition describes as contemplative prayer.

> Contemplative prayer is the poor and humble surrender to the loving will of the Father in ever deeper union with his beloved Son.

Contemplative prayer is the simplest expression of the mystery of prayer. It is a *gift*, a grace; it can be accepted only in humility and poverty. (*CCC*, 2712–2713)[27]

Joseph's prayer becomes contemplative precisely because Jesus—in the womb, as a child, as a boy, as a young man, as a partner in labor—is present to him. This presence propels Joseph ever more toward the Father, whom Joseph has come to love above all else. The ever increasing intimate union of Joseph's life with the life of the Father is the gift Mary and her child bring to this man of humble heart. Joseph's prayer is "the prayer of the child of God" (*CCC*, 2712). It is "a *gaze* of faith, fixed on Jesus" (*CCC*, 2715).

"Prayer is a mystery that overflows both our conscious and unconscious lives" (*CCC*, 2727). It is not a psychological activity by which we transcend all physical and mental voids, nor is it simply the recitation of ritual words and postures. St. Joseph opens us to the mystery of prayer by exposing it as a way of life. His determined response to God disposes him to the gift of God's own life.

Joseph teaches us that prayer doesn't come from us; we cannot manufacture it or sustain it. Prayer always has its origin in the Spirit of God, to whom we must vigilantly have recourse.

In the course of his public ministry, Jesus will have much to say about prayer. No doubt the example of his parents serves as a backdrop.

CHAPTER ELEVEN

MAN OF LABOR

Thus the heavens and the earth were finished, and all the host of them. And on the seventh day God finished his work which he had done, and he rested on the seventh day from all his work which he had done. So God blessed the seventh day and hallowed it, because on it God rested from all his work which he had done in creation. (Genesis 2:1–3)

URING MY FIRST THREE YEARS in the seminary, I worked for a pastor who was fond of saying, "Manual labor is good for the soul." While I didn't initially appreciate the wisdom of his maxim—especially while polishing brass, waxing floors, and pulling weeds—I gradually came to appreciate the perfective power of human labor. Men and women were not created to be idle but to work with creation on its journey to completeness:

> We know that the whole creation has been groaning with labor pains together until now; and not only the creation, but we ourselves, who have the first fruits of the Spirit, groan inwardly as we wait for adoption as sons, the redemption of our bodies. (Romans 8:22–23)

Our need to be productive is an inherent part of our being created in the image and likeness of the God who establishes and orders the heavens and the earth, what's visible and invisible. God is first presented as Creator, as one whose work is intentional, purposeful, and therefore good. God knows what he is about. Creation is not an accident, nor a random or capricious event.

The truth about creation is important, for it holds the answer to questions about the origin, meaning, and end of human life. In an age dominated by relativism, we must propose in new ways the truth that the dignity of our humanity is inseparable from our working "first of all to the service of persons, of the whole man, and of the entire human community" (*CCC*, 2426).

All too often human labor is regarded as nothing more than a means to an end; a job is simply a way of making money. Economics influences many of the decisions people make about what course of studies they will pursue and what occupations they will consider. There is some wisdom in this. Paul reminds us, "If any one will not work, let him not eat" (2 Thessalonians 3:10). There is a place for responsibility in providing for oneself and one's dependents.

But "Economic activity, conducted according to its own proper methods, is to be exercised within the limits of the moral order, in keeping with social justice so as to correspond to God's plan for man" (*CCC*, 2426).[28] Human labor is a fundamental dimension of man's existence, an opportunity to discover the gifts we have received from God and the fulfillment we can experience in surrendering them to his purposes. As Jesus tells his followers, "You cannot serve God and mammon" (Matthew 6:24).

GOD'S WORK

The God who acknowledged the goodness in everything he created (see Genesis 1) never stops seeing the goodness in us. The first three chapters of the book of Genesis uniquely summarize the whole of salvation history. Creation and redemption go hand in hand, because

God fashioned a world in which men and women are to be free. The Fall was a possibility from the first moment God said, "Let there be..."

"God so loved the world" that he made it open to and receptive of his very life (John 3:16). Being created "in the image and likeness" of God therefore entails being free. Human love—for God, oneself, one's neighbor, and creation—could not exist without this freedom. Yet being created in freedom also means that human beings can sin. It means we can choose whether or not God will have any place in our lives and to what extent.

Fortunately, even in the face of sin, creation was never cut off from the One who established all things according to his word. Rather, the Word through which the universe was made ensures creation's unending access to the Creator. The redemption God offers through the life, death, and resurrection of his Son is not merely a response to sin; it is an extraordinary sign of the love out of which all things came to be. Creation, the Fall, and redemption cannot be understood apart from one another. The work of redemption is part of the work of creation. Thus human work should naturally draw us into the mystery of God's generative love.

When St. Joseph receives the words of the angel, his conception of creation, sin, and redemption is significantly and wonderfully altered. The angel tells him that salvation will come about by God's entrance into this world and participation with everything created by his Word.

Joseph awakens from the dream knowing the divine origin of Mary's child. This changes the way he sees the world, which has been entrusted to man's stewardship and care (see Genesis 1:28). Joseph recognizes that dominion over creation now extends to redemption and that he will have a part to play in God's saving plan.

This in no way replaces God as the source of man's salvation. Rather it means that man has a responsibility to work out his redemption according to God's purposes (see Philippians 2:12–13). God has entrusted a great work to Joseph, one that the humble carpenter willingly accepts.

The willingness to work with God will unleash Joseph's full potential. His inherent aptitude for organization and for building is well suited to the rearing of God's Son. First and foremost, it situates Jesus in the same condition as the vast majority of people. He isn't raised with wealth, prestige, or influence but in ordinary obscurity. Many in Nazareth who hear him announce the kingdom of God will be astonished. "What is the wisdom given to him? …Is not this the carpenter?" (Mark 6:2, 3).

In his manual labor Jesus becomes part of the process by which the earth is subdued. The real experience of forming and shaping concrete objects prefigures Jesus's work of redemption: "Behold, I make all things new" (Revelation 21:5).

WORKING PARABLES

It seems to me that Joseph builds more than just a suitable home for Jesus. He also helps construct categories through which the mystery of the kingdom will be suitably articulated. I can imagine Jesus's recall of his work with Joseph when he uttered this parable:

> Every one who comes to me and hears my words and does them, I will show you what he is like: he is like a man building a house, who dug deep, and laid the foundation upon rock; and when a flood arose, the stream broke against that house, and could not shake it, because it had been well built. But he who hears and does not do them is like a man who builds a house

on the ground without a foundation; against which the stream broke, and immediately it fell, and the ruin of that house was great. (Luke 6:47–49)

Joseph's livelihood was work that required careful attention. This perhaps inspired another human expression about the mysteries of the kingdom:

> Which of you, desiring to build a tower, does not first sit down and count the cost, whether he has enough to complete it? …So therefore, whoever of you does not renounce all that he has cannot be my disciple. (Luke 14:28, 33)

Jesus's parables are filled with references to other laborers—shepherds and sowers, physicians and farmers, servants and stewards, merchants and fishermen. He "looks with love upon human work and the different forms that it takes, seeing in each one of these forms a particular facet of man's likeness with God, the Creator and Father."[29]

THE SHADOW OF THE CROSS

Perhaps the greatest aspect of human labor that Joseph could offer the Son was its association with toil. This is the inheritance of all men from Adam:

> Cursed is the ground because of you;
>   in toil you shall eat of it all the days of your life;
> thorns and thistles it shall bring forth to you;
>   and you shall eat the plants of the field.
> In the sweat of your face
>   you shall eat bread
>   till you return to the ground. (Genesis 3:17–19).

The curse that resulted from sin remains present in all human activity, whether physical or intellectual. Even though work brings pleasure and reward, it does not bring satisfaction:

> My heart found pleasure in all my toil, and this was my reward for all my toil. Then I considered all that my hands had done and the toil I had spent in doing it, and behold, all was vanity and a striving after wind, and there was nothing to be gained under the sun. (Ecclesiastes 2:10–11)

The toil that marks human life on earth resonates with the announcement of death spoken in the garden: "You are dust, and to dust you shall return" (Genesis 3:19). Jesus's unique work would necessarily include sweat, toil, and pain. His cross would pay for the disobedience that has burdened humanity from the beginning. The work in Nazareth, undertaken in complete obedience to Joseph and Mary, "both announced and anticipated the obedience of Holy Thursday: 'Not my will....'" (*CCC*, 532).[30]

Jesus was familiar with the human condition. Nazareth did not protect him from the state of fallen humanity. Rather it afforded him concrete observations of that condition, the condition he came to redeem.

Although Joseph would not witness the cross of his son, he participated in it by the sacrifice of his life, the toil of his daily work. He undertook this work in order to properly care for Mary and Jesus. In this Joseph experienced in his life a glimmer of the resurrection. Through the toil uniquely associated with the work entrusted to him by the Father, Joseph began in his unique way to build the new heavens and the new earth.

Joseph shows us that being a man of labor entails being a man of the cross. His cross was that of all who pursue peace and justice. He distinguished himself as a true disciple of Christ by willingly carrying his cross every day in the activity God called him to perform.

Joseph's work in Nazareth was a labor of love. He understood the importance of the home life of the Holy Family, and he thoughtfully and sensibly carried out the stewardship necessary. While the work of raising a child is not always easy, Joseph's task was even weightier. Mary and her son didn't need just any man; they needed this one, the one whom God had chosen for them. Joseph gave himself completely to this holy undertaking. Was he aware of what was taking place? We don't know.

We do know that every opportunity Joseph had to instruct Jesus was an opportunity to grow in the knowledge of God. Imagine being the one to teach the Son of God how to use a hammer or the one to watch anxiously the first time Jesus used a saw.

The work in Nazareth, while truly the stuff of ordinary life, was carried out by an extraordinary man. This work wasn't only for Mary and Jesus but also for all women and men united with God in Christ by the power of the Holy Spirit. Joseph continues his work for us in the Church today.

CHAPTER TWELVE

MAN OF VIRTUE

The human virtues are rooted in the theological virtues, which adapt man's faculties for the participation in the divine nature: for the theological virtues relate directly to God. They dispose Christians to live in a relationship with the Holy Trinity. They have the One and Triune God for their origin, motive, and object. (*CCC,* 1812)[31]

T HE ROMAN EMPIRE CONTROLLED MOST of the known world at the time of Jesus. The Romans had conquered the Greeks and wisely incorporated their great accomplishments into the social, political, economic, and educational structures of the empire. Living according to the Law of Moses required a tremendous amount of composure in this Hellenistic culture. Many Jews chose to make accommodations. St. Joseph had to walk a narrow line to follow what he believed rather than the beliefs of the world around him.

St. Joseph is a great example for twenty-first–century Christians. We, too, walk a narrow line, as accommodation is celebrated as the great human virtue. Today Christians are expected to abandon moral and ethical norms rooted in Scripture in favor of cultural standards that are consensus-driven. It seems that if enough people agree that a certain behavior is socially acceptable, in time just about everyone agrees to it. We have witnessed this with abortion, physician-assisted suicide, and same-sex partnerships.

In times such as these, a discussion of virtue is not easy. Once objective good is rejected in favor of subjective dispositions, society moves toward its own destruction.

St. Joseph understands the great resolve and tremendous self-possession needed to live our faith in all its vibrancy. He spent years of his life with the child who would be a sign of contradiction, "a sign that is spoken against" (Luke 2:34).

At the time in which Joseph lived the concept of virtue was well established. The Greeks understood, as did the Romans, that human life was enhanced according to a person's firm and habitual disposition toward the good. It seemed a matter of common sense that certain ways of structuring life and human interaction were destructive of human well-being, both for the individual and for the community. Both the Greeks and Romans had identified the goods that were protective of human well-being.

This way of thinking was well established among the Jews. Their covenant relationship with God was rooted in his desire for their well-being. In the commandments he gave to Moses, God had written in stone what men ought to pursue and ought to avoid in order to most fully experience their humanity: "I am the LORD your God, who brought you out of the land of Egypt, out of the house of bondage..." (see Exodus 20:2–17).

St. Joseph knew God to be the foundation of and basis for human meaning. He knew that we do not create meaning and purpose but discover them in our relationship with God. The good to which he firmly and habitually disposed himself was that revealed by the God of Abraham, Isaac, and Jacob.

St. Joseph lived a virtuous life by pursuing the good and choosing it in concrete actions, using the powers of both his mind and body. "The

moral virtues are acquired by human effort. They are the fruit and seed
of morally good acts; they dispose all the powers of the human being
for communion with divine love" (*CCC,* 1804). And Joseph knew that
a virtuous life was praiseworthy:

> I have been young, and now am old;
>> yet I have not seen the righteous forsaken
>> or his children begging bread.
> He is ever giving liberally and lending,
>> and his children become a blessing.
>
> Depart from evil, and do good;
>> so shall you abide for ever.
> For the LORD loves justice;
>> he will not forsake his saints.
>
> The righteous shall be preserved for ever,
>> but the children of the wicked shall be cut off.
> The righteous shall possess the land,
>> and dwell upon it for ever. (Psalm 37:25–29)

FOUR KEY VIRTUES

The Catholic Church identifies four "cardinal" virtues as the necessary
foundation upon which all other virtues depend; thus these are essential virtues in the pursuit of the good.

> [Wisdom's] labors are virtues;
> for she teaches moderation and prudence,
> justice and courage,
> nothing in life is more profitable for men than these.
> (Wisdom 8:7)

These four virtues—temperance (or moderation), prudence, justice, and courage (or fortitude)—govern our actions and order our passions according to reason and faith. St. Matthew describes Joseph as a "just man" (Matthew 1:19), which means he built his life upon these cardinal virtues. Although there isn't much recorded about Joseph's life, there is plenty to substantiate Matthew's claim.

First, immediately after Matthew introduces Joseph, we are a party to the carpenter's prudence (see Matthew 1:18–25). This is "the virtue that disposes practical reason to discern our true good in every circumstance and to choose the right means of achieving it" (*CCC*, 1806). Having become aware of Mary's condition, Joseph must make a decision with respect to their betrothal; "The prudent looks where he is going" (Proverbs 14:15).

Joseph applies the moral and religious principles of God's law. Even after arriving at a decision, "to send her away quietly," he takes time to "consider this." His prudence in handling this troubling situation gives God the opportunity to intervene.

We also witness Joseph's prudence by the wordless way he has been preserved in sacred Scripture. The fact that he says nothing should remind us that there is a right and a wrong time for speaking. Not everything we want to say needs to be said; some speech is a burden to others.

As St. Paul tells us, we should say "only such as is good for edifying [building others up], as fits the occasion, that it may impart grace to those who hear" (Ephesians 4:29). Prudence helps us control our speech and enables us to share the truth in love. Joseph is a perpetual reminder that, as "members of one another," we should always think carefully before saying anything, no matter how noble we consider our purposes to be.

Going back to our first encounter with Joseph in St. Matthew's Gospel, we also notice the virtue of justice operative in the choice he must make regarding Mary. "*Justice* is the moral virtue that consists in the constant and firm will to give [one's] due to God and neighbor" (*CCC*, 1807). Here Joseph has a problem. How can he give God his due, which is determined by the Law, while at the same time giving Mary hers? The Law says that an adulteress, which Mary appears to be, must be stoned, yet it also instructs Joseph to always act uprightly toward his neighbor: "You shall love your neighbor as yourself" (Leviticus 19:18).

The virtue of justice doesn't point Joseph in a particular direction. It however challenges his use of right reason in a healthy way. Whatever decision he comes to must uphold the dictates of a conscience formed by his faith in God and his adherence to the Law. Joseph doesn't try to find an exemption for himself or for Mary. Rather he comes to a solution that remains within the dictates of the Law while at the same time respecting the woman who is subject to it.

Matthew's Gospel is also a profound testimony to Joseph's fortitude, the moral virtue "that ensures firmness in difficulties and constancy in the pursuit of the good" (*CCC*, 1808). The initial period of Jesus's life is fraught with difficulties and genuine peril. The words of the angel are not a divine remedy for all future uncertainties; quite the opposite. But once Joseph knows the true nature of Mary's child, he puts aside all fear, personal and external.

Accepting the responsibility to love, protect, and care for this woman and her child demand tremendous courage, including the willingness to renounce and sacrifice his life. I imagine Joseph must have repeatedly said in the depths of his heart, "The LORD is my strength" (Psalm 118:14). Perhaps just looking at Jesus—the child, the boy, the young man—fueled Joseph's fortitude.

One ancient notion of the virtues described them as the mean between two extremes. Thus, a full and satisfying life was had by avoiding the extremes. Temperance is the virtue that best reflects this ancient description, because it is the moral virtue "that moderates the attraction of pleasures and provides balance in the use of created goods" (*CCC*, 1809). In the New Testament, St. Paul tells us that we ought "to live sober, upright, and godly lives in this world" (Titus 2:12).

St. Joseph is certainly an example of temperate living. He settled in an obscure town and attracted no attention to himself or his family. He fulfilled all the requirements of the Law: He felt comfortable traveling to Jerusalem with his wife and son—so much so that Jesus, on one occasion, actually remained behind (see Luke 2:43).

There isn't much written about the years in Nazareth, most likely because there isn't much to say. Mary and Joseph lived a well-ordered, balanced life, an ordinary life that housed the most extraordinary people—just as Christian homes are meant to do. Joseph had no greater desire than to serve Jesus and Mary, because in doing so he was serving God. Every action toward them was an expression of thanksgiving. God entrusted Joseph with the most unimaginable gift, and Joseph did everything in his power to see that the gift was returned unstained.[32]

"It is not easy for man, wounded by sin, to maintain moral balance" (*CCC*, 1811). This is the reason Christ came into the world: He is the gift of salvation.

GROWING IN VIRTUE

The action of grace upon our natural virtues is real. The virtues are forged not in the abstract but in the reality of the sacraments and God's Word. They develop as habits through our openness to God's Spirit.

St. Joseph is a superb example of this truth of our faith. Jesus's life infused Joseph's own and opened his soul to God. Joseph grew in virtue even as Jesus grew "in wisdom and in stature, and in favor with God and man" (Luke 2:52).

St. Joseph built a home for Mary and Jesus that was rooted in love. His love for God and neighbor and his love for Mary and Jesus guided all of his actions. He established a well-ordered life, a temperate life, a life of balance.

In all his years with Mary and Jesus, Joseph knew that he was being saved. He knew that he was able to persevere in serving God only because of the grace of their presence in his life. His growth in virtue correlated directly with the time he was privileged to share with them. In this he is a perfect example for Christian life. Living well is only possible to the extent that we open our hearts ever more to love God. Every day Joseph was able to recommit himself to loving God, and we can do the same. He may have experienced God's presence differently than we do, but "blessed are those who have not seen and yet believe" (John 10:29).

St. Joseph is a sign of hope that everyone who cooperates with the Holy Spirit and frequents the sacraments can become a person of exceeding virtue. A virtuous life is not the honor of a few but a promise for the many. Christ has come to adapt our faculties for participation in the divine nature. St. Joseph encourages us to let Jesus do that in us.

CHAPTER THIRTEEN

MAN OF PATIENCE

Be patient, therefore, brethren, until the coming of the Lord.
Behold, the farmer waits for the precious fruit of the earth,
being patient over it until it receives the early and the late
rain. You also be patient. Establish your hearts, for the coming
of the Lord is at hand. Do not grumble, brethren, against
one another, that you may not be judged; behold, the Judge
is standing at the doors. As an example of suffering and
patience, brethren, take the prophets who spoke in the name
of the Lord. Behold, we call those happy who were steadfast.
You have heard of the steadfastness of Job, and you have seen
the purpose of the Lord, how the Lord is compassionate and
merciful. (James 5:7–11)

E VERY CHILD, AND MORE THAN one grown-up, knows that
the longest night of the year is Christmas Eve. Anticipation
stretches each minute into an unbearably long segment of
time. Young minds eventually settle down, but not without a struggle.
When the light of Christmas morning dawns, the anxiety of the night
is quickly forgotten.

Waiting is never easy. We may move beyond the impatience associated with being young only to replace it with adult worries. In my
experience as a priest, patience is the most consistently asked-for virtue;
there never seems to be enough. If there is any at all, it waxes and wanes

like the moon moving through its phases. Patience is easily lost but not so easily found.

Worries about life are real. Will we have enough? Will our lives be secure? How will our children fare? What will we eat and drink? What will we wear? While we know that we cannot add a single moment to our lives by worrying, it's easy to succumb to anxieties about tomorrow (see Matthew 6:25–34).

No matter how reasonable our anxious concerns may seem, we need to remember that our lives matter to God. Thus when Jesus speaks about this all too common human experience, he tries to shift our focus away from self. God already knows what we need and will provide it (see Matthew 6:32). So our attention must remain fixed on the Father, to whom we are more important than the birds of the air and the wild flowers. If our hearts are firmly within his kingdom, we will be able to persevere right up to the "Day of the Lord."

This day for which each one of us waits is just like the day when God was born into our world. We eagerly await our own birth into the life of God without limitation, imperfection, weakness, fragility, or pain. We long for our common destiny, knowing that it will satisfy the deep desire of our hearts, the desire to experience fully and for all time the Love who will never let us down. We look forward to the Day of the Lord because "God's love has been poured into our hearts through the Holy Spirit who has been given to us" (Romans 5:5).

WAIT UPON THE LORD

Our Father in heaven knows how onerous waiting can be. He has therefore given us a "pledge" of the "first fruits" of our inheritance through the outpouring of the Holy Spirit. We can live in time without being controlled by it.

Paul identifies patience as a "fruit of the Spirit" (Galatians 5:22). It allows the constraints of time to fall away so that here and now we can experience life in the eternity of the Triune God. Patience disposes us toward what ultimately matters—the kingdom of God—freeing us from preoccupation with passing things. "If we hope for what we do not see, we wait for it with patience" (Romans 8:25). The failures and disappointments of others, the world, and ourselves do not determine our sentiments or behavior. Patience calms the mind and keeps the heart firmly in the Father's love.

Patience is a necessary requirement of love. God's love for us has been revealed through his forbearance. He does not wish that any one of us should perish (see 2 Peter 3:9) but rather that we "come to the knowledge of the truth" (1 Timothy 2:4). We can say that, in a sense, God waits for each one of us as "the farmer waits for the precious fruit of the earth" (James 5:7).

The seed of faith that has been planted in our hearts is watered by the early and late rains of the sacraments and the Scriptures. Slowly it grows until it has become the largest of plants (see Matthew 13:32), though we "know not how" (Mark 4:27). God's love is never forceful or controlling; it doesn't manipulate or restrict us. Rather God's love is like yeast. It acts upon our nature and causes us to rise to new life (see Matthew 13:33).

I think of St. Joseph's life as a sort of documentary on patience. Even before the visitation of the angel, he knew a good deal about waiting. With his people he shared the hope that God would once again restore them and gather them to himself. He earnestly looked forward to the coming of the Messiah, without knowing when he would come or how he would fulfill God's promises.

St. Joseph knew that waiting was an integral part of life lived in covenant with God, one that required trust and confidence. Like the best of his ancestors, he was firmly convinced about the future glory of the people of Israel.

> I believe that I shall see the goodness of the LORD
>   in the land of the living!
> Wait for the LORD;
>   be strong, and let your heart take courage;
>   yea, wait for the LORD! (Psalm 27:13–14)

Then Joseph's waiting seems to come to an end. An angel tells him that the woman to whom he is betrothed has conceived a child by the power of the Holy Spirit (see Matthew 1:20). This child is the fulfillment of the promise (1:23). Through him, salvation will come to God's people, because he will free them from their sins.

It may seem impossible that Joseph would awaken from such a dream and accept it as divine intervention. Yet the angel's words resonated with the hopes of his people.

One period of waiting concludes, and another begins. Joseph will need more than natural patience to carry out his responsibilities before the Lord. Only by remaining focused on what is in front of him—namely, Mary and her child—will he be free from anxious thinking. They will calm his heart and steady his resolve. They will keep Joseph grounded in time rather than its slave. They are the promise in its most nascent form.

Joseph learned what every Christian eventually comes to realize: Waiting is a significant part of being in a covenant relationship with God. Joseph waited as we should. He kept his focus on what was required of him: to care for and water the seed of redemption that had been planted in his life. He did not try to make circumstances conform to his own ideas. Rather he brought his gifts and talents into whatever situation he faced and used them to address the needs of Mary and Jesus.

PRACTICE MAKES PERFECT

Through Joseph we learn that patience is an active virtue. Patience is only possible to the extent that what will later be determines how we act in the here and now. Patience indicates the extent to which the future has spilled over into the present and the present into the future. Patience is a disposition we foster by confidence in God. It enables us to recognize the real difficulties and problems that may be part of the moment without collapsing in anxiety or despair.

In practicing patience we share the disposition of the prophets, the apostle James tells us (see James 5:10). They preached God's promises without knowing if they would be the ones to see them completely fulfilled.

Imagine Joseph's wonder at meeting Simeon in the Temple. This man has been "looking for the consolation of Israel" (Luke 2:25). The Holy Spirit has told the older man that he will see the Christ in his lifetime, and Simeon's response has been righteousness and devotion. Simeon and Joseph come face-to-face, sharing the experience of seeing God's salvation present in Mary's child. And that is enough for these two men.

In petitioning God for more patience, we should ask to become more confident in him and thus more engaged in his kingdom. All too often prayers for patience are focused on our own needs. But patience doesn't "fix" the way we feel about what's happening or what will happen. It centers the heart on God, thereby reorienting the way in which we interact with others and with reality.

Patience is a sign that the theological virtues are operative in our lives. When faith, hope, and charity take root in the human heart, all anxious worrying ceases.

> The theological virtues...are infused by God into the souls of the faithful to make them capable of acting as his children and of meriting eternal life. They are the pledge of the presence and action of the Holy Spirit in the faculties of the human being. (*CCC*, 1813)

These virtues make it possible for us to live in this world with our hearts and minds set on the world that will never end.

As far as we know, Joseph had little or no experience of Jesus's public ministry. He would not live to see Jesus accomplish his redemption. Mary stood at the foot of the cross (see John 19:26); Joseph seems to have been spared that horror. He accepted the salvation God offered him in the daily sacrifices of his life with Christ.

St. Joseph's life beautifully portrays patience as a fitting disposition of true faith. He is the kind of man Jesus hoped to find when he returned in glory to the earth (see Luke 18:8). Every day God was merciful to Joseph, because every day Joseph was able to spend time with Jesus and his mother. There is no other explanation for this privilege than the fact that God looked upon Joseph with love.

Joseph teaches us to accept the gifts we have been given. Mary and Jesus were God's pure gifts to him, greater than Joseph could have ever imagined or hoped for. Their lives radically transformed his. Through Mary and Jesus, Joseph was truly "baptized" into the life of God.

We who are baptized are similarly gifted with the presence—indeed, the indwelling—of the Trinity.

Baptism…makes the neophyte…an adopted son of God, who has become a "partaker of the divine nature," member of Christ and co-heir with him, and a temple of the Holy Spirit.

The Most Holy Trinity gives the baptized sanctifying grace…. (*CCC,* 1265–1266)[33]

Each of us has everything necessary to live in God. By our active participation within the company of those who follow Christ, this new life is sustained and deepened. We should not look to what we think we need, however noble and good our desires may be, but to what God has already given. We must accept God's redemptive power in our lives, however God chooses to make it known. We turn our gaze from what others seem to have, from what is lacking in our lives, and accept with gratitude everything that God has given us.

I heard Mother Teresa of Calcutta tell people repeatedly not to come to Calcutta: "There is one Mother Teresa of Calcutta, me. You stay where you are and become the person God has asked you to be."[34] This perfectly sums up the life of St. Joseph. He accepted his role in the drama of salvation and will persevere in that role right up to the Day of the Lord. He does so because he is a patient man, engaged with the necessities of the present even as he looks forward to what is coming.

St. Joseph helps us accept and develop the Spirit's gift of patience. He helps us see the pearl of great price that has been entrusted to our care. He helps us let go of whatever else may have a possessive hold on our hearts (see Matthew 19:21).

CHAPTER FOURTEEN

MAN OF THE CHURCH

Now the company of those who believed were of one heart
and mind, and no one said that any of the things which he
possessed was his own, but they had everything in common.
And with great power the apostles gave their testimony to the
resurrection of the Lord Jesus, and great grace was upon them
all. (Acts 4:32–33)

THE DESCRIPTION OF THE EARLY Church seems to depict
something much different from our contemporary experience. Where two or three are gathered in the name of the
Lord today, you'll most likely have two or three different ideas about
what it means to be a member of the Church. God is surely present, but
so too are people's varied ideas about what it means to be a community
and a believer. From liturgy to ministry, from discipline to doctrine, it's
painfully clear that the community of believers don't seem to be of one
heart and mind.

After two thousand years of bearing witness to the resurrection of
the Lord Jesus, the community of believers has been through a lot.
There have been splits and schisms, heresies and reforms, inquisitions
and disputations, councils and corruption. "The new life received in
Christian initiation has not abolished the frailty and weakness of
human nature, nor the inclination to sin that tradition calls *concupiscence*" (*CCC*, 1426).[35] Yes, we are a fractious group.

Yet this points toward a truth about the Church that is sometimes forgotten: The Church is a *life*, despite its rifts and dissensions.[36] In order to truly understand what it means to be a community of believers, we have to live this life!

THE CHURCH'S MISSION

The task of bearing witness to the resurrection is only possible for someone who recognizes the resurrection as a real event. I consider arguments about whether or not a man can be raised from the dead to be, in the end, a waste of time. If a virgin and an old lady can have babies, then "with God nothing will be impossible" (Luke 1:37).

I also find it somewhat pointless to argue about the validity of the Church's sacramental claims. These claims hinge on whether or not Jesus rose from the dead. The witness of the apostles was not to an idea or a theory, and certainly not to an institutional structure, but to a factual event. That event quite literally rocked their world! When Jesus rose, "there was a great earthquake; for an angel of the Lord descended from heaven and came and rolled back the stone, and sat upon it" (Matthew 28:2).

The community of early believers engaged in a life that was fueled by the reality that Jesus was dead and three days later was bodily alive! (see Luke 24:39; John 20:27). A person engaged in the life that is the Church must bear witness to this event, because it is in fact what makes the individual's life worth living. The resurrection is the reason the Church is a life.

St. Paul states this eloquently:

> If Christ has not been raised, then our preaching is in vain and your faith is in vain.... If Christ has not been raised, your faith is futile and you are still in your sins.... If for this life only we

have hoped in Christ, we are of all men most to be pitied.

But in fact Christ has been raised from the dead, the first fruits of those who have fallen asleep. (1 Corinthians 15:14, 17, 19–20)

On the road to Damascus, Paul met the risen Christ, who showed himself to be one with the community Paul was persecuting (see Acts 9:3–6). His transformation was dramatic. From that moment on he could say, "It is no longer I who live but Christ who lives in me; and the life as I now live in the flesh I live by faith in the Son of God, who loved me and gave himself for me" (see Galatians 2:20).

The way to be part of a community of believers of one heart and mind is life in Christ; this is the life the Church is. This does not come about from mere duty, nor can it come simply by accepting all that the Church proposes about God and humanity. It can only happen to the extent that the individual can bear witness to the resurrection. If I cannot personally attest to the resurrection as a fact, then I am not yet living the life that is the Church.

How does this historic event become a reality for a particular congregation? Someone must bear witness to the truth of God become man, crucified, died, buried, and raised. "How are men to call upon him in whom they have not believed? And how are they to believe in him of whom they have never heard? And how are they to hear without a preacher?" (Romans 10:14). Pamphlets and programs, books and Bible studies are important, but most importantly, persons need to bear witness. Why? This was the method God used: He chose to become a man! This is how he made himself known.

Thus, an encounter with someone for whom the truth of God in Jesus Christ has become the driving force of his or her identity is the greatest source of conversion. In the presence of one whose life is wholly ordered around the resurrection of Jesus from the dead, the Holy Spirit inspires the heart and enlightens the mind about the truth of the person of Jesus. When this happens, the community can be of one mind.

THE DOMESTIC CHURCH

As father of the Church, St. Joseph is first and foremost the father of a life! This is the beautiful and yet rarely appreciated story of Nazareth. Three people lived a life together! They were interested in and attentive to one another. They were engaged with each other and with the world around them.

Theirs was not a life of obdurate pious solitude. They ate and slept and cleaned and laughed and shopped and shared and prayed and worked. They were of one heart and mind, because they were all serving God, albeit in different ways. They had each been profoundly touched by the presence of God, and each bore witness to the truth of God's presence.

Joseph certainly fathered this life in the home at Nazareth. There God gathered Joseph and Mary to himself around the person of his Son. The Church had its genesis in this first "Christian" family. This is the life that Jesus spread in his public ministry. He gathered people together: "This gathering is the Church, 'on earth the seed and beginning of [the] kingdom'" (*CCC,* 541).[37] This is the life that would be born from the pierced side of Jesus. "I, when I am lifted up from the earth, will draw all men to myself" (John 12:32).

As head of the family, Joseph established the structure for the life they shared with one another and with God, and he nourished and sustained that life.

Life in Nazareth is a model for the life of the Church. It was a life centered on God in the person of Christ. There Jesus had everything needed for his life as God become man. We, too, have everything we need in order to live in him. St. Joseph is Father of the Church because he is the custodian of the life we live in Christ. We should be eager to entrust the Church to his care.

Joseph encourages us to adopt a proper attitude toward life in the Church. We don't experience this life only on Sundays. The Church as a life means that every moment of my existence bears witness to the resurrection. At work, in the supermarket, at home, at school, or wherever I am and in whatever situation I face, my life is Church. It is the presence of Christ in me penetrating and punctuating time and circumstances with the truth of the Father's love.

The Church isn't the building in which we gather with the community of believers or the sacraments we celebrate, although both have their place. It is the whole of my life lived in communion with Christ's own. St. Joseph helps me keep sight of the fact that my life is the place Christ has chosen to meet me and to dwell (see John 1:14). The Incarnation not only changed his life but became his life.

Thus St. Joseph helps us pursue our shared destiny and the truth of our being. He longs to raise us to full maturity in the faith. He wants us to understand what the Incarnation means: God has sent his Word into human history. In order to know this Word become flesh, we need to be familiar with Jesus's human life, the things he said and did, and how he died.

St. Joseph, as father of the Church, is a champion of sacred Scripture. He prayed the psalms with his family, reflected on the sacred writings of his people, and attended the customary religious festivals. In each of these situations, the presence of Jesus and Mary gave greater height and depth and breadth to his awareness of the kingdom. In turn, he constantly drew closer to both Jesus and Mary.

Our familiarity with the Word does the same for us. It draws us into a deeper knowledge of the Savior and his work. Thus we can bear witness to the resurrection.

The gift of the life in Nazareth was a gift meant for everyone. Mary and Joseph shared in Jesus's "mission, joy, and sufferings" long before he left home to take up his public ministry. Mary would see Jesus's ministry to the end. God revealed the mystery of his kingdom in Nazareth through the communion of love Jesus shared with Mary and Joseph. This communion would extend to all in "a mysterious and real communion between his own body and ours: 'He who eats my flesh and drinks my blood abides in me, and I in him'" (*CCC*, 787).[38]

Jesus longs to have all people abide in him, just as he abided in love in the home at Nazareth.

> Abide in me, and I in you. As the branch cannot bear fruit by itself, unless it abides in the vine, neither can you, unless you abide in me. I am the vine, you are the branches. He who abides in me, and I in him, he it is that bears much fruit, for apart from me you can do nothing. (John 15:4–5)

"By communicating his Spirit, Christ mystically constitutes as his body those brothers of his who are called together from every nation" (*CCC*, 788).[39] The community of believers is therefore a unified body with Christ as its head (see Colossians 2:18–19). Through baptism we are united with his life and thus with the life of every other member.

Joseph lovingly encourages us to be taken up into the mysteries of Jesus's life, so that we may be glorified with him (see Philippians 3:21; Romans 8:17). Joseph continues to serve the Father's plan of redemption by serving Christ's body, the Church. He longs to safeguard the life that is the Church, because it is one with the very life he raised to manhood.

As father of the Church, Joseph is rightly the father of each of her members. Joseph's relationship with us is personal: He doesn't relate generically to the whole body but according to our diversity as her members (see 2 Corinthians 12:7). He extends to us the same loving, guiding, parental care he gave to Jesus, according to each of our needs.

This is perhaps best understood in terms of his relationship with Mary. While her "role in the Church is inseparable from her union with Christ and flows directly from it" (*CCC*, 964), that role was strengthened and supported by her relationship with Joseph. He was able to provide for her as she gave birth to Jesus and raised him. He did the work for which the Father chose and equipped him. The Spirit "apportions to each one individually as he wills" (1 Corinthians 12:11).

Joseph's heart still beats with the Sacred Heart. Thus it beats for the entire community of believers, as with one heart and mind they bear witness to the resurrection.

CHAPTER FIFTEEN

SHEPHERD, PROTECTOR, AND GUARDIAN

In the presence of God who gives life to all things, and of Christ Jesus who in his testimony before Pontius Pilate made the good confession, I charge you to keep the commandment unstained and free from reproach until the appearing of our Lord Jesus Christ; and this will be made manifest at the proper time by the blessed and only Sovereign, the King of kings and Lord of lords, who alone has immortality and dwells in unapproachable light, whom no man has ever seen or can see. To him be honor and eternal dominion. Amen. (1 Timothy 6:13–16)

THE PASSAGE ABOVE IS PART of a longer letter St. Paul wrote to a young presbyter who had been given the responsibility of leading a local church—what today we call a diocese. The ministry entrusted to Timothy was understandably significant. As the head of the community, it would be his responsibility to both safeguard and serve the sacramental, spiritual, and material needs of the people under his pastoral protection. He was expected to "aim at righteousness, godliness, faith, love, steadfastness, gentleness" in order to "take hold of eternal life" (1 Timothy 6:11, 12).

Timothy had become the spiritual "father" of these people, through the imposition of hands and the gift of the Holy Spirit (see 1 Timothy

4:14). Thus it would be his duty to show people how "to behave in the household of God" (1 Timothy 3:15).

As the Church continued to grow, Peter and the other apostles appointed men such as Timothy to share their apostolic ministry. This was a means of ensuring that people had access to the teaching the apostles had received (see 1 Corinthians 11:23–25) and the sacramental, spiritual, and material support they needed. The office Peter and the apostles received was "destined to be exercised without interruption by the sacred order of bishops" (*CCC*, 862),[40] whose task it is to shepherd the people of God entrusted to their care.

Like Timothy, the bishops are to be fathers to their people, especially to the priests and deacons who participate in their episcopal ministry. With vigilance they are to safeguard the gift of God that has been given to the faithful, through the sacrament of baptism, and strive always to protect people from the wolves who prowl in sheep's clothing, looking to strike.

A PATRON FOR BISHOPS

The fatherhood of the bishop, rooted in the call of Peter and the twelve, is foremost a ministry of charity. Jesus sent the Spirit upon the apostles to ordain them to carry out in time the ministry he had received from his Father: to reconcile the world to God. Following Jesus is the essence of Christian charity.

On the night before he died, Jesus washed his disciples' feet and told them that he had given them a model, "that you also should do as I have done to you" (John 13:15). Jesus's act of love reveals the definitive pattern for loving God and loving one's neighbor:

> God is love, and he who abides in love abides in God, and
> God abides in him. In this is love perfected with us, that we

may have confidence for the day of judgment, because as he is so are we in this world. (1 John 4:16–17).

St. Joseph is a fitting model for every bishop, for God has entrusted a precious life into each bishop's care; the life that is the Church. Just as Joseph accepted his responsibility to care for God's Son, so each bishop should regard each life entrusted to his care as the object of his vocation. Joseph's sensitivity to the mission of Jesus—in every prayer he taught, every chore he assigned, and every instruction he gave at the workbench—should inspire every bishop's effort to shepherd and protect the family of God.

Religious instruction is more than the dissemination of information. The content should be wedded to a vigorous and enthusiastic witness to the resurrection. This passionate, active, and attentive witness begins in the local church with the bishop, the father of the spiritual family, and extends to all those who assist him in his ministry. All ministers of the Gospel have distinct personalities, gifts, and expertise; all should use what they have to bear witness to the resurrection. Joseph is a patron to assist them in letting Christ show forth in their lives.

The bishops' task of governing is really no more complicated than this: Our common destiny must drive all decisions about liturgy, disciplines, structures, codes, and canons. Whatever interferes with the building up of the body of Christ should be thrown into the depths of the sea (see Matthew 18:6).

Our era in the history of the Church has its unique challenges and demands; we must meet these with a view toward ultimate necessities. We cannot allow the prevailing currents of culture to shift the house of God off the solid foundation of Peter's confession of faith. Governing the body of Christ is not a political or juridical act but first and foremost a spiritual charge. The Dogmatic Constitution on the Church states:

The bishops, as vicars and legates of Christ, govern the particular Churches assigned to them by their counsels, exhortations and example, but over and above that also by the authority and sacred power which indeed they exercise exclusively for the spiritual development of their flock in truth and holiness.[41]

Joseph is perfectly suited to guide bishops in their task of governing. The good shepherd goes in search of the lost and brings them home (see Luke 15:4). This calls for a willingness to protect them, even to the point of laying down one's life for them (see John 10:11).

Joseph received his spiritual charge the night the angel came to him in a dream. The flock entrusted to his care was small but significant. Joseph put his all into protecting them. Scripture indicates that he died before Christ's passion, perhaps because this son was no longer to be protected from cruelty and death. Joseph's task was done.

GUARDIAN OF VIRGINS

In a special way St. Joseph safeguards the members of the Church who are most vulnerable in our society; their unique conditions demand exceptional care. Chief among these are virgins, immigrants, and children. They move Joseph's heart in a particular way because of the Virgin entrusted to his care, his own status in a foreign land, and the child he welcomed into his home.

From apostolic times Christian virgins and widows, called by the Lord to cling only to him with greater freedom of heart, body, and spirit, have decided with the Church's approval to live in the respective states of virginity or perpetual chastity 'for the sake of the Kingdom of heaven' (*CCC,* 922).[42]

Through their consecration these women "are betrothed mystically to Christ, the Son of God, and are dedicated to the service of the Church"

(*CCC*, 923).[43] What man could possibly understand better the choice these women have made to be a transcendent sign of the Church's love of Christ than a man whose spouse remained a virgin? Joseph experienced in his life both the great good of marriage and esteem for virginity for the sake of the kingdom, as it was embodied in Mary. Her virginity is "*the sign of her faith,* 'unadulterated by any doubt,' and of her undivided gift of herself to God's will" (*CCC*, 506).[44]

The words of the angel, shrouded in a dream, exposed Joseph to the "divine work that surpasses all human understanding and possibility" (*CCC*, 497).[45] It is a message foretold in Scripture: "Behold, a virgin shall conceive and bear a son, and shall call his name Immanuel" (Isaiah 7:14). Joseph accepted in faith the fact that "God in his saving plan wanted his Son to be born of a virgin" (*CCC*, 502).

How eager, then, is Joseph to protect the women who by choice and consecration have united their lives in a special way to the life of Mary. How eager he is to help them courageously live and work, according to their distinct gifts, as a leaven in the world. The courageous stance these women take today is no less daring and mysterious than was Mary's: "Let it be to me according to your word" (Luke 1:38).

While Joseph cherishes the heroic nature of any life lived for Christ alone, he has a special affinity for these daughters of the Church. Their lives are signs that contradict the coarse modes of femininity that emasculate modern men, demean genuine womanliness, and assault the sacredness of human sexuality. Joseph stands by the wise virgins of the Church as they wait with lighted lamps for the coming of the Bridegroom (see Matthew 25:1–10; Revelation 14:4; 1 Corinthians 7:32.) At the same time he helps all in the Church better understand the special "bond with Christ" they enjoy (*CCC*, 1619).

GUARDIAN OF IMMIGRANTS

St. Joseph also accompanies immigrants as they make their way to foreign lands with hopes of a better life and genuine human freedom. He knows that moving to a new country is not easy. In his time it was the tyrannical act of a frightened ruler that caused Joseph to flee. He left family and friends he loved and a way of life he knew to go to Egypt, a land that had once been a place of slavery for his people. There he and his family would be strangers.

Egypt was more a place of exile than a place to build a new life. Joseph probably longed for home. So he can empathize with those who must leave their country and whose hearts share similar longings.

The lives of immigrants can be filled with anxiety and fear. Even if they successfully make it to the place of their dreams, there are obstacles to overcome. Assimilation, essential for stability and prosperity, can take time and real effort, especially when it requires learning a new language and new customs. And there is no guarantee of acceptance. The difficulties can be so overwhelming that doubt creeps in about the initial decision to travel to a new land. Immigrants may waver in their resolve to stay and their ability to say, "I belong."

The Church is a diverse body spread throughout the world; she knows firsthand, through her members, the plight of the immigrant. Every missionary is an immigrant. From Pentecost to our own day, many have left the security of home for the purpose of announcing the truth of God's love and the kingdom in which the Father has prepared a room for every one of us.

Even after the Gospel took hold in new territories and among new peoples, the migration of men and women from one land to another continued. New methods of transportation and greater access to them made it easier for large groups of people to leave unfavorable conditions in their native countries for the opportunity and prosperity offered in another. Often groups of immigrants were not only of the same ethnic background but also of the same faith.

In the United States, Catholic immigrants from many different countries became neighbors with men and women who shared their faith but not their country of origin. The parish should have welcomed all Catholics, bringing diverse immigrant communities together as a first step toward integration into the society at large. In most instances, the parish was better suited to assist those of shared national origin in adjusting to the customs and culture they encountered here. In my own diocese, there were often conflicts between Catholics of different nationalities, because each immigrant community was competing with others for employment, housing, security, and success.

American Catholics today can experience the universality of the Church in the peoples of different countries, customs, cultures, and languages who have migrated here. Every parish that once was identified by national or ethnic origins should be a place that warmly accepts Catholics from different lands with their unique traditions. The ancestors of these communities were once immigrants—frightened, unsure, and in need. Christ came into the world an immigrant, and he is still present in the world as an immigrant. "I was a stranger and you welcomed me" (Matthew 25:35). St. Joseph can be of great assistance in parish efforts to become warm and welcoming to the stranger.

LET THE CHILDREN COME

Christ is also present in children. In fact, he tells us that we must become like children if we are to enter the kingdom of heaven (see Matthew 18:3), for God has revealed his mysteries to the childlike (see Matthew 11:25).

Children naturally hold a special place in the life of the Church. They remind us of Christ, who came into the world as we all do—naked, hungry, and in need. Children recall our own lost innocence. By their purity of heart they can push us toward the Spirit of God. Thus Christ can be formed in us and "the mystery of Christmas [can] be fulfilled in us" (*CCC*, 526).[46]

Children are signs not only of our adoption into the family of God but of his enduring benevolence. For "what father among [us] if his son asks for a fish, will instead of a fish give him a serpent? Or if he asks for an egg, will give him a scorpion?" (Luke 11:12). Since we are God's children now, we should have the same trust and confidence that form the natural disposition of every child. His love comes to us with gentleness and care.

Sadly, we live at a time in which the innocence of childhood has been shattered by social horrors and psychological aberrations. Over the past thirty years, we have heard more about child abductions and child sexual abuse. There is currently an organized movement to lower the age of legal consent in order to facilitate adult-child sex. Public education now includes sexual education in the curriculum of primary school students, with little thought given to their fragility and vulnerability. Our sex-obsessed culture is actively destroying the purity of children in a push to alleviate adult guilt.

The innocence of children is assaulted on many fronts, but none is more appalling than that of abortion. For forty years unborn children have been threatened and destroyed in our nation. What does this say about those who are born? Society seems to say that their existence has no innate value. It would make no difference if they hadn't been brought to term.

Today more than ever, children need St. Joseph to guard and protect them from the constant assaults on their innocence, their purity, their dignity, and their very lives. The Church must have regular recourse to this man whose singular responsibility was to protect God's Son. For Joseph can see in today's attitudes and actions toward children the shadow of the tetrarch who sought to kill the child Jesus. Joseph can hear Rachel mourning as her children are put to death in the womb (see Matthew 2:18; Jeremiah 31:15).

St. Joseph is a wonderful patron of the Church's efforts to keep her children safe from clerical sexual abuse. He longs to preserve all children in the grace of the Nazareth home. He knows how susceptible they are to the evils that surround them. He is also a patron of those who work in any capacity to reorient society toward recognizing the good that children inherently are.

St. Joseph was charged by God to care for his only begotten Son. From his place within the bosom of the Trinity, he serves God still, shepherding those who call upon his name, guarding those who have accepted life in Christ and strive to live it faithfully, and protecting the most vulnerable among us.

Joseph sees in all members of Christ's body the child he helped raise, the boy he instructed, and the man with whom he labored. This quiet man should not be forgotten. We should invoke his intercession, invite him into our homes, and enshrine him in our hearts. Each of us needs guidance and protection as we grow "from one degree of glory to another" (2 Corinthians 3:18) and look forward to the coming of the King of kings and Lord of lords.

THE COMMUNION OF SAINTS

Therefore, since we are surrounded by so great a cloud of witnesses, let us also lay aside every weight, and sin which clings so closely, and let us run with perseverance the race that is set before us, looking to Jesus, the pioneer and perfecter of our faith, who for the joy that was set before him endured the cross, despising the shame, and is seated at the right hand of the throne of God.

Consider him who endured from sinners such hostility against himself, so that you may not grow weary or faint-hearted. (Hebrews 12:1–3)

T HE CHURCH HAS LONG UNDERSTOOD that the community of Christ's body extends to those who "have gone before us marked with the sign of faith."[47] The body of the faithful includes both the living and the dead: those awaiting fullness of life within the eternity of God's love here (the Church Militant) and in purgatory (the Church Suffering), as well as those already beholding "in full light God himself triune and one, exactly as he is" (the Church Triumphant) (*CCC*, 954).[48] As St. Paul reminded the Christians of Corinth, "By one Spirit we were all baptized into one body" (1 Corinthians 12:13).

"All, indeed, who are of Christ and who have his Spirit form one Church and in Christ cleave together" (*CCC*, 954, quoting *Lumen Gentium* 49; see Ephesians 4:16). Even now the living and the dead are united in a mystical communion that allows their relationships not only to continue but even to deepen. The first preface for the Mass of Christian Burial reassures those who mourn that "life is changed, not ended."[49] Our hope for eternal life is therefore a hope for more than reunion with our deceased loved ones; our hope is to experience the communion we already share dimly with them. In heaven we will know and be known completely, without any limitations or imperfections. "For now we see in a mirror dimly, but then face to face. Now I know in part; then I shall understand fully, even as I have been fully understood" (1 Corinthians 13:12).

FRIENDS IN HIGH PLACES

The Church's teaching on the communion of saints assures us: Through the power of the Holy Spirit, baptism unites us in a communion of love that "neither death, nor life, nor angels, nor principalities, nor things present, nor things to come, nor powers, nor height, nor depth, nor anything else in all creation" is able to destroy (Romans 8:38–39). We have died and risen with Christ! The only limits to experiencing the fullness of life that Christ offers are those we set for ourselves, in thought, in word, and in deed.

To live fully the communion that Christ offers us as members of his body, we must be open to the rich treasury of his love, which is "reinforced by an exchange of spiritual goods" (*CCC*, 955). We must also be open to the men and women who facilitate this exchange. Being receptive to the whole of Christ's body ensures our faithfulness to the deepest vocation of the Church.

The whole company of men and women experiencing the eternity of God's love want us to encounter Christ in such a way that our lives become open to the full, rich possibilities that exist within the mind of the Father. The saints want us to live in the light of the truth that only Christ reveals, experiencing now what it means to live the joy and freedom of the children of God. The saints don't yearn to be our friends; they already are our friends. From within the Trinitarian communion, they long to help us experience more deeply the inexhaustible splendor of God's love.

They do this first and foremost by helping us see more clearly who we are. They offer their lives as mirrors by which we can reflect upon our own. If we grant them a place in our lives, they will point out our need to change and give us the encouragement to do so. Like good friends they stand by us, constantly assuring us that where they are we might likewise be. They never condemn, belittle, or reject us, although they do challenge and correct us.

Through, with, and in Christ, the saints are truly present to us. They are not merely figures from the past whose life histories help us become holy. Nor do they exist on some higher plane to which we have no access. Christ brings us into communion with them. Let us accept and experience the gift of friendship he makes possible.

By sharing fully in Christ's mission to unite all things in himself, the saints serve and glorify the Father. They do not hinder or replace the work of Christ; rather they subsist as a perpetual part of that work.

Like all good friendships, our relationships with the saints enhance our lives. Their presence establishes a healthy awareness of our inherent dignity in virtue of being created in God's image and likeness. Being true friends with the saints is a safeguard against pernicious heresies that devalue human existence.

The help the saints give is similar to what Jesus gave the Samaritan woman. When he sat and spoke with her at Jacob's well, his intention wasn't to make her feel bad. He offered her friendship. The encounter presented a new chance to satisfy the desires of her heart.

Pointing out what the woman had done was a necessary part of the encounter. The man asking for a drink of water knew that the woman needed perspective on her life. Jesus's presence, along with his words, acted as a catalyst to get the woman to appreciate herself as a valuable human being. This new awareness was so incredibly freeing for her that, without any thought as to what others might think, she returned to her town and enthusiastically announced her discovery.

The saints also tell us everything we have ever done. They do this by the example of their lives. Their histories can point out our need to change, inspire us, assure us of God's love, and humble us. Sometimes their stories provide the blessing of humor, which drives the devil away. If we, like the Samaritan woman, remain steadfastly receptive, we will find this experience healing and refreshing.

We should welcome in our lives those who not only want what's best for us but help us to see it. We should have as friends those who are willing to say even what we may not want to hear. Good friends increase our self-awareness, encourage and support us, and never ask us to do anything hurtful or unhealthy. We should welcome in our lives all those who long to help us become the person God has created us to be.

THE COMPANY WE KEEP

Human friendship is often presented in the Gospels as an instrument of Christian discipleship. In the Gospel of John, Philip encourages his friend Nathanael, using the words Jesus spoke to the followers of John the Baptist, "Come and see" (John 1:39). Nathanael agrees to follow his friend's advice, most likely out of curiosity: "Can anything good come out of Nazareth?" (John 1:46).

Jesus doesn't disappoint! Upon meeting him, Nathanael is immediately struck by what Jesus says: "Behold, an Israelite indeed, in whom is no guile!" (John 1:47). How can a man Nathanael's never met know him? Jesus builds on Nathanael's curiosity, and by the end of the encounter, Nathanael is hooked by the Fisher of Men. Jesus's promise of greater things may confirm Nathanael's decision to follow him, but it follows Nathanael's confession, "Rabbi, you are the Son of God! You are the King of Israel!" (John 1:49).

We all long to be known; we all long to have at least one person actually grasp who we are. Friendships fulfill this longing. And the saints are good friends.

Once we have discovered ourselves in Christ, it is nearly impossible to walk away. His words of everlasting life are more than theological insights and moral imperatives; they uniquely and personally touch our hearts. Those "with ears to hear" find the innate desires of their hearts fully satisfied.

While the initial moment of Christian discipleship arises from our desire to be known, only Christ can sustain its momentum. The saints encourage us, by their example and prayer, to stay focused on him. Our friendships with them renew our convictions and give us courage to persevere in Christ's love. The things they show us and the lessons they teach us fix our gaze firmly on the person of Christ.

As "the mediator of a new covenant" (Hebrews 9:15), Christ allows the saints to help us receive our promised inheritance, just as he allowed Philip to help Nathanael obtain his. The saints are not all-knowing. Their knowledge of us originates in Christ and expands as our friendships with them grow. What they share with us is never general or impersonal.

My experience of St. Joseph will never be exactly the same as someone else's. There may certainly be similarities, because Joseph has particular qualities that all of us admire and particular patronages that we may seek. But our experiences with him are uniquely our own, just as all friendships are unique.

The saints experienced in their lives the greater things that Jesus promised Nathanael. They also draw our attention to the concrete circumstances and situations in which "greater things" are being revealed in our lives. Our friendships with them are great gifts offered to us by Christ. These gifts help us realize the goodness, truth, and beauty of our humanity in Christ, because their own humanity exists within the life of God.

In order to foster a genuine friendship with the saints, we need to be somewhat familiar with their lives. There are many wonderful books and websites that tell us about the saints, especially the more modern ones. I encourage you to get to know these men and women in glory. Perhaps you'll find a special friend among them.

LITANY OF ST. JOSEPH

THERE ARE MANY SAINTS BEHOLDING God himself of whom we know very little. St. Joseph, of course, is one of them. I have found that an easy way for me to meditate upon his life and get to know him is to pray his litany. I find that the titles by which he is described place the whole of his life in relief. They bring to mind questions about him and about myself as a follower of Christ. Just as the repetition in the rosary frees my mind to reflect upon Christ's life, Joseph's litany allows me to reflect upon his many virtues, which are the most important things for me to know about him and to imitate.

Since my mother first introduced me to St. Joseph, I have used the following litany to come to know better the man who raised Jesus. It is my hope that it might help you do the same.

Lord, have mercy on us.

Lord, have mercy on us.

Lord, have mercy on us.

Christ, have mercy on us.

Christ, hear us.

Christ, graciously hear us.

God, the Father of Heaven,

have mercy on us.

God the Son, Redeemer of the world,

have mercy on us.

God the Holy Ghost,

   have mercy on us.

Holy Trinity, one God,

   have mercy on us.

Holy Mary,

   pray for us.

Holy Joseph,

   pray for us.

Noble Son of the House of David,

   pray for us.

Light of the Patriarchs,

   pray for us.

Husband of the Mother of God,

   pray for us.

Chaste Guardian of the Virgin,

   pray for us.

Foster-father of the Son of God,

   pray for us.

Sedulous Defender of Christ,

   pray for us.

Head of the Holy Family,

   pray for us.

Joseph most just,

   pray for us.

Joseph most chaste,

   pray for us.

Joseph most prudent,

   pray for us.

Joseph most valiant,

   pray for us.

Joseph most obedient,

   pray for us.

Joseph most faithful,

   pray for us.

Mirror of patience,

   pray for us.

Lover of poverty,

   pray for us.

Model of all who labor,

   pray for us.

Glory of family life,

   pray for us.

Protector of virgins,

   pray for us.

Pillar of families,

   pray for us.

Consolation of the afflicted,

   pray for us.

Hope of the sick,

   pray for us.

Patron of the dying,

   pray for us.

Terror of the demons,

   pray for us.

Protector of the holy Church,

   pray for us.

Lamb of God, you take away the sins of the world,
   have mercy on us.
Lamb of God, you take away the sins of the world,
   have mercy on us.
Lamb of God, you take away the sins of the world,
   have mercy on us.

1. Quoting Vatican II, *Dei Verbum*, 15.
2. See Pope Benedict XVI, *Deus Caritas Est*, 5.
3. Quoting *Lumen Gentium*, 11.
4. Quoting *Lumen Gentium*, 10.
5. Quoting Matthew 18:10; Psalm 103:20
6. Cf. Isaiah 66:13; Psalm 131:2.
7. Cf. Psalms 27:10; Ephesians 3:14; Isaiah 49:15.
8. See Romans 5:19.
9. Quoting Pope Paul VI at Nazareth, January 5, 1964, Feast of the Holy Family.
10. Quoting *Lumen Gentium*, 36.
11. See *Catechesi Tradendae*, 5.
12. *De gratia Dei et de peccato originali* 24, 25, Corpus Scriptorum Ecclesiasticorum Latinorum.
13. Quoting *Dei Verbum*, 10; cf. 1 Timothy 6:20; 2 Timothy 1:12–14 (Vulgate).
14. Quoting Hebrews 10:23; Titus 3:6–7.
15. See *Lumen Gentium*, 1.
16. Quoting *Gaudium et Spes*, 39.
17. Quoting the *Roman Catechism*, Preface, 10; see 1 Corinthians 13:8.
18. See Matthew 5:17–19.
19. *Deus Caritas Est*, 18.
20. Quoting Matthew 5:48.
21. Quoting Luke 14:33; see Mark 8:35; Luke 21:4.
22. Quoting *Lumen Gentium*, 42.
23. Quoting *Gaudium et Spes*, 58.
24. Quoting Tertullian, *De oratione* 1: PL 1, 1155.

25. See St. Augustine, *De diversis quaestionibus octoginta tribus* 64, 4: PL 40, 56.
26. See John 9:27; *Lumen Gentium*, 68–69.
27. See *CCC,* 2709–2719.
28. See *Gaudium et Spes* 64.
29. *Deus Caritas Est*, 18.
30. Quoting Luke 22:42.
31. See 2 Peter 1:4.
32. "With your family and friends to help you by word and example, bring that dignity unstained into the everlasting life of heaven" *Rite of Baptism*, p. 60.
33. Quoting 2 Corinthians 5:17; 2 Peter 1:4; Cf. Galatians 4:5–7; Cf. 1 Corinthians 6:15; 12:27; Romans 8:17; Cf. 1 Corinthians 6:19.
34. Mother Teresa, quoted by the author, who worked with her personally for many years.
35. Cf. Council of Trent (1546): DS 1515.
36. For a fuller explanation of the Church as a life, see Luigi Guissani, *Why the Church?* trans. Viviane Hewitt, Luigi Guissani (Montreal: McGill-Queens University Press, 2001).
37. Quoting *Lumen Gentium,* 5.
38. Quoting John 6:56.
39. Quoting *Lumen Gentium,* 7.
40. Quoting *Lumen Gentium,* 20.
41. Vatican II, *Lumen Gentium,* Dogmatic Constitution on the Church, 27, in Austin Flannery, *Vatican Council II, Volume 1: The Conciliar and Post Conciliar Documents* (New York: Costello, 1998), pp. 382–383.
42. Quoting Matthew 19:12; see 1 Corinthians 7:34–36; John Paul II, *Vita consecrate*, 7.

43. Quoting CIC, canon 604.
44. Quoting *Lumen Gentium* 63; see 1 Corinthians 7:34–35.
45. Cf. Matthew 1:18–25; Luke 1:26–38.
46. See Galatians 4:19.
47. Eucharistic Prayer I.
48. Quoting *Lumen Gentium,* 49; cf. Mt 25:31; 1 Corinthians 15:26–27; Council of Florence (1439): DS 1305.
49. *Roman Missal,* Preface of Christian Death I.

About the Author

Fr. Gary Caster has worked as a high school chaplain, religion teacher, and director of campus ministries at Bradley University, Eureka College, Illinois State University, and Illinois Wesleyan University. The author of several books, including *The Little Way of Lent* and *The Little Way of Advent*, he also has written and produced shows for EWTN. He is the Catholic chaplain at Williams College in Williamstown, Massachusetts, and he continues to lead retreats and parish missions.